The Society for Theatre Research

THE OPERAS OF RICHARD STRAUSS

IN BRITAIN

1910-1963

THE OPERAS OF
RICHARD STRAUSS
IN BRITAIN
1910-1963

ALAN JEFFERSON

PUTNAM

First published 1963
for the Society for Theatre Research by
PUTNAM AND CO LTD
42 Great Russell Street London WC1

Printed in England by
William Clowes & Sons Ltd
London and Beccles

'. . . alles zergeht wie Dunst und Traum.'

HUGO VON HOFMANNSTHAL

FOREWORD

AN EXAMINATION of all the performances of the operas of a single composer in one country alone is research with a microscope, and perhaps a book of exactly this kind has never been written before. The Society for Theatre Research is particularly glad to sponsor Mr. Alan Jefferson's work as an English contribution to the celebration of the centenary of Richard Strauss, born at Munich on June 11, 1864.

The following abbreviations have been used in the footnotes: *Recollections*, for Richard Strauss, *Recollections and Reflections*, English edition, 1949; *Correspondence*, for *The Correspondence between Richard Strauss and Hugo von Hofmannsthal*, English edition, 1961; *Beecham*, for *A Mingled Chime. Leaves from an Autobiography by Sir Thomas Beecham, Bart.*, 1944.

V. C. CLINTON-BADDELEY

General Editor of Publications
for The Society for Theatre Research

London, 1963

AUTHOR'S PREFACE

SOURCES OF information for opera researchers are mostly limited to standard works of reference or scattered among theatre programmes, gramophone record catalogues and musical publications. The Society for Theatre Research asked me in 1961 to compile a Handbook of the Operas of Richard Strauss's Operas Performed in Great Britain. This I have done, both for the Strauss novice and the Strauss expert.

The information comes from the contemporary Press (in which not a little social history is reflected), and *every* performance in the British Isles is noted. Lack of space has prevented the inclusion of complete cast-lists, but all principal voices and the conductors are taken from programmes which (with a very few exceptions) I have handled.

For the sake of clarity *Ariadne auf Naxos* with *Le Bourgeois Gentilhomme* is treated as a separate work from the revised version of the opera, and I have called them Ariadne I and II according to convention. Thus my total of Richard Strauss operas is sixteen, instead of the usual fifteen, although, as will be evident, only ten of these sixteen have yet been performed in Great Britain.

ASH, Surrey.   ALAN JEFFERSON
May 1963

ACKNOWLEDGEMENTS

I AM extremely grateful to the following persons and organisations who willingly helped to unearth the facts, large and small, without which my work would have come to a standstill. They comprised, among others, the precise casts and dates of over 475 performances in fifty-three years; the unpublished alterations to casts (those called out before the curtains, over an expectant hush, by a gentleman in evening dress); the disproving of some good stories, and the discovery of better ones; the details of those mystery tours undertaken by the long-extinct Denhof Company in 1912 and 1913; and of the more recent but equally undocumented excursions of the Covent Garden Opera throughout the Midlands and North of England, Scotland and Wales (but never Ireland), in the 30's, 40's and 50's.

I have thus discovered that research depends not only upon patience, but also upon the generosity of: Sir David Webster, for making available information from the Archives of the Royal Opera House; Miss Gillian Jones for helping me there; Mr. Harold Rosenthal, Keeper of these Archives, Editor of *Opera*, a private collector and the principal source for English opera research. Mr. Rosenthal has most generously answered my innumerable requests and has lent me material otherwise unobtainable, over the past year and a half. Furthermore, he has looked through my manuscript and has pointed out a number of errors which I have now been able to avoid and correct. I am deeply grateful to him.

Mr. William Mann has kindly allowed me to reprint his programme notes for the London premières of *Liebe der Danae* and *Capriccio*, and gave me very useful advice on German sources of information about these two operas. Mr. Arthur Jacobs has allowed me to reproduce his copyright synopsis of *The Silent Woman*. Mr. Norman Del Mar has, from the fund of his musical and scholarly wisdom, been unstinting in his immediate supply of answers to my questions, particularly about *Ariadne I* in 1950.

Mme. Miriam Licette, Mr. Aylmer Buesst and Mr. Norman Allin all helped to set me on the right path towards uncovering details of the Opera Tours in 1931-1932; Mr. Harold Barrett produced programmes of these tours and told me a lot about his career as assistant to Charles Moor at Covent Garden between the wars; and Miss Joan Cross and Mr. Parry Jones kindly produced facts to clear up nagging problems. Miss June Dandridge verified cast changes at Glyndebourne, and Brother Brendan of the Catholic Central Library generously gave up a day to do research on the *Golden Rose*.

Thanks are also due to Mr. David Alexander of Sadler's Wells for verifying cast changes and supplying programmes; to Mr. Ernest Lindgren of the National Film Archive for allowing a special showing of the 1926 *Rosenkavalier* Film, and to the Misses Davies and

Minich of this organisation for personally arranging it. I am also deeply grateful to Mr. George Nash and his Staff at the Enthoven Collection in the Victoria and Albert Museum, not only for having given me *carte blanche* among their files, but also for their interest in my project. Also to Miss Jean Daniels, B.B.C. Music Publicity Department, for information about the television production of *Salome*.

The Archivist of the Hamburg State Opera and the Director of the Salzburg Festival have kindly given me much help and I wish to thank them.

And the Librarians of the Public Libraries of Aberdeen, Birmingham, Cardiff, Croydon, Edinburgh, Glasgow, Kingston-upon-Hull, Leeds, Liverpool, Manchester, Newcastle upon Tyne, and Sheffield all responded most generously to my requests for information about Opera Tours since 1912, thus enabling me to make this book representative of Britain, rather than of London alone.

A. J.

CONTENTS

The Operas of
RICHARD STRAUSS
in Britain 1910-1963

THE OPERAS OF RICHARD STRAUSS

Opera	Opus No.	Place and Date of Première		British Première
Guntram	25	Weimar	May 10, 1894	—
Feuersnot	50	Dresden	November 21, 1901	July 9, 1910
Salome	54	Dresden	December 9, 1905	December 8, 1910
Elektra	58	Dresden	January 25, 1909	February 19, 1910
Der Rosenkavalier	59	Dresden	January 26, 1911	January 29, 1913
Ariadne auf Naxos I	60	Stuttgart	October 25, 1912	May 27, 1913
Ariadne auf Naxos II	60	Vienna	October 4, 1916	May 27, 1924
Die Frau ohne Schatten	65	Vienna	October 10, 1919	—
Intermezzo	72	Dresden	November 4, 1924	—
Die ägyptische Helena	75	Dresden	June 6, 1928	—
Arabella	79	Dresden	July 1, 1933	May 17, 1934
Die schweigsame Frau*	80	Dresden	June 24, 1935	November 20, 1961
Friedenstag†	81	Munich	June 24, 1938	—
Daphne†	82	Dresden	October 15, 1938	—
Die Liebe der Danae	83	Salzburg	August 14, 1952	September 16, 1953
Capriccio	85	Munich	October 28, 1942	September 22, 1953

* In 1938 Beecham hoped to produce *The Silent Woman* at Covent Garden, but because the libretto was by a Jew, and the opera was consequently banned in Germany, too many casting difficulties were involved and the plan was abandoned.

† In 1939 Beecham was forced to cancel an unannounced intention to invite the Dresden Opera Company to perform *Friedenstag* and *Daphne* at the London Music Festival of that Summer.

Of the sixteen operas by Richard Strauss, ten have been performed in Great Britain. It was nine years before the first one arrived from Germany, yet within the next three years five operas had been heard in London and two in the Provinces, thanks entirely to Thomas Beecham.

The first 'Strauss year' was 1953 when six different works could be heard between January and December in London, owing to the visit of the Bavarian State Opera to Covent Garden with their two novelties and one rare revival.

Rosenkavalier is the hardy perennial; *Salome* and *Elektra* have more frequently been in the Covent Garden repertory during the last ten years, and *Ariadne II* in the Glyndebourne repertory since the last war.

SOURCES OF THE OPERAS

The greatest source of inspiration comes from Greek mythology. Von Hofmannsthal's intellect enabled him both to present the world's oldest dramas in a new framework, and to play tricks with mythology: *Ariadne* is the best example.

From the Greek: *Elektra, Ariadne auf Naxos*; basis for *Liebe der Danae, Daphne* and *ägyptische Helena.*

From a Flemish Legend, *The Quenched Fires of Audenarde*: *Feuersnot*

From Oscar Wilde: *Salome*

From a suggestion of Alexander Ritter and the condition of being 'over-awed' by Wagner: *Guntram*

From Louvet de Couvray: *Rosenkavalier*

From Ben Johnson's *Epicœne*: *The Silent Woman*

From contemporary events: *Intermezzo* (domestic) *Friedenstag* (political)

From an original 'magic fairy tale' by Hugo von Hofmannsthal: *Frau ohne Schatten*

From a sketch for a comedy called *The Cabby as Count* by Hugo von Hofmannsthal: *Arabella*

From an eighteenth-century play by Casti, elaborated by Clemens Krauss and Richard Strauss: *Capriccio*

TITLES OF THE OPERAS

The titles of fourteen out of the sixteen operas depend upon women for their names: *Salome*, *Elektra*, *Ariadne I* and *II*,[1] and *Arabella*; *The Silent Woman*, *Die Liebe der Danae*; in *Der Rosenkavalier*, the title role is sung by a (mezzo) soprano *en travesti*; *Feuersnot* has in its title a German pun wherein *Feuer* means not only fire but also sexual ardour. This refers to the heroine Diemut. *Capriccio* is an intellectual title for an intellectual opera in which the central character is a woman.

Of the six operas not so far performed in Great Britain, three are *Die Frau ohne Schatten* (another pun: the woman is not only without shadow, but also without issue); *Die ägyptische Helena* and *Daphne*; *Intermezzo* is an autobiographical work about Strauss's *wife* and himself.

[1] In the Prologue the central figure of the 'Composer' is sung by a soprano *en travesti*.

THE OPERAS IN BRITAIN

RICHARD STRAUSS'S OPERAS IN BRITAIN BY SEASONS

All performances sung in German unless otherwise stated

1910	Covent Garden *Elektra*	Winter Season February 19–March 19 February 19 British Première	9 Perfs.
1910	His Majesty's Theatre, London *Feuersnot*	The Thomas Beecham Opéra Comique Season, May 12–July 30 July 9 British Première in English	5 Perfs.
1910	Covent Garden *Elektra* *Salome*	Autumn Season October 3–December 31 December 8 British Première	4 Perfs. 10 Perfs.
1912	Denhof Opera Company on Tour *Elektra*	February 26–March 29 Opera in English February 29 World Première in English	

	HULL	2 Perfs.
	MANCHESTER	2 Perfs.
	LIVERPOOL	2 Perfs.
	LEEDS	2 Perfs.
March 26 Scottish Première	GLASGOW	1 Perf.

1913	Covent Garden *Rosenkavalier* *Elektra* *Salome*	Winter Season January 29–March 8 January 29 British Première	8 Perfs. 3 Perfs. 4 Perfs.

1913	His Majesty's Theatre,
	London
	  With Beerbohm Tree's
	  Company in *Le Bourgeois
	  Gentilhomme* in English
	Ariadne I
		May 27–June 7
		
		Opera in German
		May 27 British Première
			8 Perfs.

1913	Denhof Grand Opera Company on Tour	September 15–October 4 Opera in English		
	Elektra		BIRMINGHAM	1 Perf.
	Rose Bearer	September 20 World Première in English		
			BIRMINGHAM	3 Perfs.
	Elektra		MANCHESTER	1 Perf.
	Rose Bearer		MANCHESTER	2 Perfs.
1913	Denhof/Beecham Grand Opera Company on Tour	October 13–November 22 Opera in English		
	Rose Bearer		SHEFFIELD	2 Perfs.
	Elektra		SHEFFIELD	1 Perf.
	Rose Bearer		LEEDS	1 Perf.
	Rose Bearer		LIVERPOOL	2 Perfs.
	Rose Bearer		MANCHESTER	1 Perf.
	Elektra		NEWCASTLE UPON TYNE	1 Perf.
	Rose Bearer		NEWCASTLE UPON TYNE	1 Perf.
	Rose Bearer	November 17 Scottish Première		
			EDINBURGH	2 Perfs.
	Elektra		EDINBURGH	1 Perf.
1914	Theatre Royal, Drury Lane	Summer Season May 2–July 25		
	Rosenkavalier			6 Perfs.
1924	Covent Garden	Summer Season May 5–July 1		
	Salome			4 Perfs.
	Rosenkavalier			6 Perfs.
	Ariadne II	May 27 British Première of 2nd version		2 Perfs.
1925	Covent Garden	Summer Season May 18–July 10		
	Rosenkavalier			5 Perfs.
	Elektra			2 Perfs.
1927	Covent Garden	Summer Season May 2–June 24		
	Rosenkavalier			5 Perfs.
1929	Covent Garden	Summer Season April 22–June 28		
	Rosenkavalier			5 Perfs.
1931	Covent Garden	Summer Season April 27–July 3		
	Rosenkavalier			4 Perfs.

1931	Covent Garden Opera Company on Tour *Rosenkavalier*	October 26–December 19 Opera in English		
			GLASGOW	2 Perfs.
			EDINBURGH	2 Perfs.
			LIVERPOOL	2 Perfs.
			BIRMINGHAM	2 Perfs.
1932	Covent Garden Opera Company Spring Tour *Rosenkavalier*	January 25–March 19 Opera in English January 25 First perf. in English in London		
			STREATHAM HILL	3 Perfs.
			GOLDERS GREEN	3 Perfs.
			HALIFAX	3 Perfs.
			MANCHESTER	3 Perfs.
1932	Covent Garden Opera Company Autumn Tour *Rosenkavalier*	October 24–December 10 Opera in English		
			GLASGOW	2 Perfs.
			EDINBURGH	2 Perfs.
			HALIFAX	2 Perfs.
			MANCHESTER	1 Perf.
1933	Covent Garden *Rosenkavalier*	Summer Season May 1–June 9		3 Perfs.
1934	Covent Garden *Arabella*	Summer Season April 30–June 15 May 17 British Première		4 Perfs.
1936	Covent Garden *Rosenkavalier*	Summer Season April 27–June 12		3 Perfs.
1936	Covent Garden *Rosenkavalier* *Ariadne II*	Visit of Dresden State Opera November 2–13		2 Perfs. 1 Perf.
1936/7	Covent Garden *Salome*	Winter Season December 26, 1936–January 23, 1937		3 Perfs.
1938	Covent Garden *Rosenkavalier* *Elektra*	Summer Season May 2–June 17		4 Perfs. 2 Perfs.
1938/9	Sadler's Wells *Rosenkavalier*	Season October 17, 1938–May 20, 1939 in English		7 Perfs.
1947	Covent Garden *Rosenkavalier*	Season January 6–July 5 in English		10 Perfs.

1947	Covent Garden Opera Tour *Rosenkavalier*	August 18–October 25 in English		
			GLASGOW	2 Perfs.
			LIVERPOOL	2 Perfs.
			MANCHESTER	2 Perfs.
			BIRMINGHAM	1 Perf.
			CROYDON	2 Perfs.
1947	Covent Garden *Salome*	Visit of Vienna State Opera September 16–October 4		3 Perfs.
1947	Drury Lane *Ariadne I* (excerpts)	London Strauss Festival October 12, 1947		1 Perf.
1947/8	Covent Garden *Rosenkavalier*	Season October 31, 1947–June 5, 1948 in English		6 Perfs.
1948/9	Covent Garden *Rosenkavalier*	Season September 29, 1948– June 5, 1949 in English		4 Perfs.
1949/50	Covent Garden *Rosenkavalier* *Salome*	Season September 29, 1949–March 3, 1950 in English in English		4 Perfs. 6 Perfs.
1950	Covent Garden *Rosenkavalier*	Season May 3–July 1 in English		1 Perf.
1950	King's Theatre Edinburgh *Ariadne I*	Edinburgh Festival August 20–September 10 August 21 Scottish Première Play in English, Opera in German		9 Perfs.
1950/1	Covent Garden *Rosenkavalier* *Salome*	Season October 19, 1950–February 28, 1951 in English in English		8 Perfs. 2 Perfs.
1951	Covent Garden Opera Spring Tour *Rosenkavalier*	March 12–31 in English		
			EDINBURGH	1 Perf.
			MANCHESTER	1 Perf.
1951	Covent Garden *Salome*	Season April 12–July 7 in English		2 Perfs.
1951	Covent Garden Opera Autumn Tour *Rosenkavalier*	July 9–28 in English		
			LEEDS	2 Perfs.
			LIVERPOOL	1 Perf.

1951/2	Covent Garden	Season October 22, 1951–February 22, 1952		
	Rosenkavalier	in English		5 Perfs.
	Salome	in English		1 Perf.
1952	Covent Garden	February 25–April 5		
	Opera Tour	in English		
	Rosenkavalier	February 26 Welsh Première of a Strauss opera	CARDIFF	1 Perf.
	Salome	in English and German February 28 Welsh Première	CARDIFF	1 Perf.
	Salome	in English	MANCHESTER	1 Perf.
	Salome	in English March 19 Scottish Première	GLASGOW	2 Perfs.
	Rosenkavalier	in English	BIRMINGHAM	1 Perf.
	Salome	in English	BIRMINGHAM	1 Perf.
1952	Covent Garden	Season April 14–June 28		
	Salome	in English		2 Perfs.
	Rosenkavalier	in English		3 Perfs.
1952	King's Theatre, Edinburgh	Edinburgh Festival August 17–September 6 Visit of Hamburg State Opera		
	Rosenkavalier			3 Perfs.
1952/3	Covent Garden	Season October 23, 1952–February 15, 1953		
	Rosenkavalier	in English		4 Perfs.
1953	Covent Garden	March 9–April 18		
	Opera Tour	in English		
	Rosenkavalier		GLASGOW	1 Perf.
			LIVERPOOL	1 Perf.
			MANCHESTER	2 Perfs.
			BIRMINGHAM	2 Perfs.
1953	Covent Garden	Season April 20–July 11		
	Rosenkavalier	in English		6 Perfs.
	Elektra			4 Perfs.
1953	Opera House, Glyndebourne	Season June 27–July 6		
	Ariadne II			8 Perfs.
1953	Covent Garden	Visit of Bavarian State Opera September 15–26		
	Arabella			5 Perfs.
	Die Liebe der Danae	September 16 British Première		4 Perfs.
	Capriccio	September 22 British Première		2 Perfs.

13

1953/4	Covent Garden	Season October 19, 1953–February 13, 1954	
	Salome	in English	3 Perfs.
1954	Covent Garden	Season April 20–July 24	
	Elektra		3 Perfs.
	Rosenkavalier	in English	3 Perfs.
1954	Opera House, Glyndebourne	Season June 10–July 27	
	Ariadne II		6 Perfs.
1954	King's Theatre, Edinburgh	Edinburgh Festival August 22–September 11 Glyndebourne Opera Company	
	Ariadne II	August 24 Scottish Première	6 Perfs.
1954/5	Covent Garden	Season October 25, 1954–February 26, 1955	
	Rosenkavalier	in English	5 Perfs.
1955	Covent Garden	Season April 18–July 24	
	Salome	in English	4 Perfs.
1955	Royal Festival Hall, London	Season September 13–23 Visit of Stuttgart State Opera	
	Elektra		2 Perfs.
1955/6	Covent Garden	Season October 17, 1955–February 18, 1956	
	Rosenkavalier	in English	6 Perfs.
1956	King's Theatre, Edinburgh	Edinburgh Festival August 19–September 8 Visit of Hamburg State Opera	
	Salome		5 Perfs.
1957	Opera House, Glyndebourne	Season June 11–August 13	
	Ariadne II		8 Perfs.
1957/8	Covent Garden	Season October 28, 1957–February 26, 1958	
	Elektra		4 Perfs.
1958	Covent Garden	Season April 2–May 31	
	Elektra		4 Perfs.
1958	Opera House, Glyndebourne	Season May 27–July 31	
	Ariadne II		8 Perfs.
1958/9	Covent Garden	Season October 31, 1958–February 28, 1959	
	Rosenkavalier	in English	6 Perfs.
	Salome	in English	5 Perfs.

1959	Covent Garden	March 2–28	OXFORD	2 Perfs.
	Opera Tour	in English	MANCHESTER	2 Perfs.
	Rosenkavalier			

| 1959 | Covent Garden | Season April 1–July 18 | | |
| | *Rosenkavalier* | in English | | 3 Perfs. |

| 1959 | Opera House, Glyndebourne | Season May 28–August 16 | | |
| | *Rosenkavalier* | | | 13 Perfs. |

1959/60	Covent Garden	Season October 28, 1959–July 16, 1960		
	Salome			3 Perfs.
	Rosenkavalier			5 Perfs.
	Elektra			4 Perfs.

| 1960 | Opera House, Glyndebourne | Season May 24–August 16 | | |
| | *Rosenkavalier* | | | 13 Perfs. |

| 1960/1 | Covent Garden | Season October 19, 1960–June 17, 1961 | | |
| | *Rosenkavalier* | | | 4 Perfs. |

1961	Covent Garden	March 20–April 15	OXFORD	1 Perf.
	Opera Tour		COVENTRY	1 Perf.
	Rosenkavalier		MANCHESTER	2 Perfs.
			LEEDS	1 Perf.

| 1960/1 | Sadler's Wells | Season October 5, 1960–April 22, 1961 | | |
| | *Ariadne II* | in English | | 8 Perfs. |

1961/2	Covent Garden	Season September 14, 1961–June 17, 1962		
	The Silent Woman	in English		
		November 20 British Première		7 Perfs.

| 1961/2 | Sadler's Wells | Season September 27, 1961–June 17, 1962 | | |
| | *Ariadne II* | in English | | 5 Perfs. |

| 1962 | Opera House, Glyndebourne | Season May 21–August 19 | | |
| | *Ariadne I* | Play in English, Opera in German | | 11 Perfs. |

1962/3	Covent Garden	Season September 7, 1962–June 29, 1963		
	Rosenkavalier			4 Perfs.
	Rosenkavalier			5 Perfs.

| 1963 | Opera House, Glyndebourne | Season May 22–August 18 | | |
| | *Cappriccio* | | | 10 Perfs. |

ELEKTRA

ELEKTRA

ELEKTRA WAS RICHARD STRAUSS'S fourth opera in order of composition but the first to be performed in London. It is thus necessary to bear in mind that *Salome*, which preceded it, and which is also about a lustful woman, dissuaded the composer from pursuing *Elektra* as a subject. As he says, 'At first I was put off by the idea that both subjects were very similar in psychological content, so that I doubted whether I should have the power to exhaust this subject. . . . Both operas are unique in my life's works; in them I penetrated to the uttermost limits of harmony, psychological polyphony (Klytemnestra's dream) and of the receptivity of modern ears.'[1]

Strauss visited the Deutsche Theater in Berlin at the end of 1905 to see the tragedy of *Elektra* by the young Austrian poet Hugo von Hofmannsthal. Although Strauss was searching for a comedy to be the basis for the libretto of a new opera he was at once impressed by the musical opportunities which this play offered[2]; and 'which Hofmannsthal bred, by Freud, out of Sophocles', as Eric Blom put it.

As von Hofmannsthal had unsuccessfully attempted in 1900 to interest Strauss in a collaboration, he was only too glad to go as far as he could to meet the composer's demands, and to sidetrack him from other wild ideas such as *Cesare Borgia*, *Semiramis* and *Saul and David*.

Correspondence between them started from the end of 1907 in what is now seen to be the typical manner. The opera was first performed in Dresden on January 25, 1909.

The Story of the Opera

THE SCENE is laid in the courtyard of the palace at Mycenae, and here one finds Elektra, in rags, lamenting her father, King Agamemnon, who has been murdered by his Queen, the jewel-covered Klytemnestra and her lover Aegisthus. The guilty woman believes that sacrifices will induce the gods to remove the horrors by which she is haunted, but she is terrified as to what the future will bring her. Then comes news that Elektra's brother, Orestes, is dead, an announcement which intensifies her grief. But happily the news is false. Orestes appears, and, urged on by Elektra, he enters the palace bent on vengeance. The harrowing shrieks of Klytemnestra and Aegisthus indicate the culmination of the tragedy, for Orestes has killed them with the hatchet with which his father had been murdered.

[1] *Recollections*, pp. 154–5.

[2] *Elektra*, the play, was written by von Hofmannsthal in 1903 and performed in translation at the New Theatre, London, in a double bill with Yeats's *Deirdre of the Sorrows* at a matinée on Nov. 27, 1908. Mrs. Patrick Campbell was Elektra and Deirdre.

Elektra dances triumphantly—she is satisfied—and then she collapses, dead. As the curtain falls, one hears her younger sister Chrysothemis, calling for Orestes.

(Synopsis from Programme of May 26, 1925.
No synopses in programmes of 1910 or 1913.)

In early January 1910, the young Mr. Thomas Beecham (he was thirty) announced a season of light opera from February 19 to March 15 (later March 19) at Covent Garden. There were only three familiar operas in the repertoire, and among the other five was *Elektra*. Despite this, advance booking and interest in the project were so satisfactory that before the season opened another was announced for at least thirteen weeks in the autumn.

Towards the opening date of the season and the first *Elektra* in Britain, public interest was increased, there was a black market in tickets, and the Press took advantage of the more sensational aspects of the plot. Beecham slyly records 'some of this journalistic fever, which my advertising manager assured me was of untold value, occasioned embarrassment now and then to the theatre staff'.[1]

These 'advance notices' were partly caused by the fact that *Elektra* had been performed (in French) at the Manhattan Opera House, New York, in February, so that 'the false colouring of the preliminary gossip must have hindered the right appreciation of the work'.

Then 'after rehearsals of unprecedented length and severity, after preparations which extended to the tiniest detail of the stage picture, the *Elektra* of Richard Strauss was produced at Covent Garden on February 19, 1910' (*Observer*), in the presence of the King and Queen, the Prince and Princess Henry of Prussia, and many notable society people and musicians.

Mr. Beecham cannot but have been grateful that the 'sensational peculiarities' attributed to *Elektra* from the other side of the Atlantic caused a full house and many disappointed people unable to get in on the first night. For once the general public found they were—if only temporarily—interested in opera.

Royal Opera House, Covent Garden

First Beecham Opera Season 1910
February 19, 1910 (British première) for nine performances in German

	February 19, 23, 26, 1910	March 3, 1910	March 5, 1910	March 12, 15, 1910	March 17, 19, 1910
Elektra	Walker	Fassbender	Fassbender	Walker	Krull
Chrysothemis	Rose	Rose	Rose	Rose	Petzl
Klytemnestra	Bahr-Mildenburg	Metzger	Bahr-Mildenburg	Bahr-Mildenburg	Bahr-Mildenburg
Orestes	Weidemann	Weidemann	Weidemann	Bender	Austin
Aegisthus	D'Oisly	D'Oisly	D'Oisly	D'Oisly	D'Oisly
Conductor	Beecham	Beecham	Beecham	Strauss	Beecham

Costumes designed by Comali and executed by B. J. Simmons & Co., Covent Garden
Stage Manager: Herr Wirk

[1] *Beecham*, p. 90.

20

The only serious critic who appears to have given *Elektra* a bad notice was Ernest Newman, writing for *The Nation*. The daily and Sunday newspapers, the glossy magazines and the public were all overwhelmed at the 'triumph', 'superb production', 'brilliant production', 'superb performance', 'remarkable success', and so on. The reputation of American music critics was said to have been killed.

Those who had heard the opera in Dresden conceded a change of view on certain aspects of the score which admitted fresh and altogether revealing subtleties to the ear at a second hearing; and others were quick to appreciate that where ugly sounds occurred they emphasised an ugly character or an ugly happening upon the stage.

Mr. Beecham was especially singled out for the highest praise, 'of whom not his warmest admirers could have expected so notable an achievement'; and 'clearly it is to him we have to look for that modern progress in operatic matters that will bring London into line with the great Continental capitals' (*Daily Telegraph*).

The principal singers were headed by Miss Edyth Walker, an American, who had appeared at Covent Garden in 1908 as a memorable Isolde. She was able to sustain the heavy role of Elektra, who remains on stage for the last 75 of the 100 minutes of this one-act opera, and is singing for most of the time.[1] Her acting was said to be 'splendid in force and conviction' (*Morning Post*).

Frau Mildenburg, as the ravaged Klytemnestra, gave a performance 'of amazing lucid power' (*Daily Mail*), 'with her heavy eyelids and awkward gait' (*The Times*), and Frances, Rose as the only example of 'normal womanhood' gave 'a very beautiful representation of Chrysothemis' (*Daily Telegraph*). At the dramatic climax Herr Weidemann, as Orestes—and at a vocal climax, too, since no male voice has yet coloured the score—was 'dignified' although a trifle 'stodgy'.

At the fall of the curtain there was dead silence, and then a thunder of applause, which continued for over ten minutes while the cast and conductor appeared and reappeared. Finally Mr. Beecham appeared with a laurel wreath 'as big as a life-buoy' and he must have been grateful to know that Queen Alexandra remained seated to applaud him after the rest of the Royal Party had left the Box.

For the fourth performance there was a new Elektra in Zdenka Fassbender, and Ottilie Metzger sang Klytemnestra.

Shaw attended the fifth performance, after which he entered into a long wrangle with Ernest Newman, then music critic of *The Nation*, who had expressed great dislike of the work. Shaw says: 'I owe it to Germany to profess my admiration of the noble beauty and power of Frau Fassbender's Elektra. Even if Strauss's work were the wretched thing poor Mr. Newman mistook it for, it would still be worth a visit to Covent Garden to see her wonderful death dance. . . . The other German artists, notably Frau Bahr-Mildenburg, shewed great power and accomplishment; but they have received fuller acknowledgement,

---

[1] The arduous nature of the part may be appreciated from a story of the first Elektra in New York (Mme. Mazarin) who fainted after the opening performance. On recovering she stated that she expected to faint after every one, adding, 'It is worth it!'

whereas we should not have gathered from the reports that Frau Fassbender's performance was so extraordinary as it actually was. . . . She was a superb Elektra.'[1]

Strauss came to London to conduct two performances of *Elektra* (at a fee of £200 each[2]) at the time when he was busy scoring Act II of *Rosenkavalier*. 'In accordance with his promise, Dr. Richard Strauss arrived in London last week to conduct *Elektra* at Covent Garden. On the Friday he rehearsed the orchestra and on the Saturday conducted his much discussed work. . . . The delicacy of his hands was particularly noticeable as he conducted. At the end of the performance he received ovation after ovation and appeared on the stage with the principals. After the tenth "call" he reappeared with Mr. Beecham. . . .'[3] Queen Alexandra was again present at the seventh performance, and received Strauss and Beecham afterwards. The three principal women were as on the first night but Paul Bender was a new Orestes (he was later to become a famous Ochs). Of Bender, von Hofmannsthal said: 'he does not mind how much one tells him and, as an actor, possesses a rich store of shades of expression'.[4]

A very good eye-witness account, written at the performance on March 12, of Strauss's appearance and manner in the pit, appeared in the *Daily Mail*: 'The tall, pale man with the dome-shaped head, the huge, smooth brow, the steel-blue eyes, sat slightly bent forward with a glow on his delicate features which are those of a lyric poet rather than of a musical giant. His thin, long hand held the tapering baton like a pen. His head was immobile; only his eagle eyes flashed from time to time towards Elektra or Chrysothemis on the stage, towards the strings at his feet around him, the brass on his right, the percussion on his left. His elbows seemed riveted to his body. The sobriety of his gestures was striking. The baton did not cleave the air with fantastic arabesques; he seemed a mathematician writing a formula on an imaginary blackboard neatly and with supreme knowledge.'

At the eighth and ninth performances Beecham returned to the pit and the Dresden creator of Elektra, Anny Krull, appeared. Her conception of the part was not as big as Edyth Walker's. Louise Petzl(-Perard) was considered vocally to be a better Chrysothemis than Rose. Among the eight interpreters of Elektra who Strauss remembered thirty-two years later with particular gratitude[5] were Krull, Walker, Fassbender and Plaichinger.

Royal Opera House, Covent Garden
Second Beecham Opera Season 1910
October 4, 1910, for four performances in German

	October 4, 14, 1910	October 24, 1910	November 26 (Mat.) 1910
Elektra	Walker	Plaichinger	Plaichinger
Chrysothemis	Petzl-Perard	Petzl-Perard	Petzl-Perard

[1] George Bernard Shaw, *How to Become a Music Critic*, Ed. by Dan H. Lawrence, 1960, p. 263.
[2] £1,000 in 1963 purchasing power.
[3] *Illustrated London News*, March 19, 1910, p. 425. Article headed 'A much discussed visitor . . .'
[4] *Correspondence*, p. 74.
[5] *Recollections*, p. 157.

	October 4, 14, 1910	October 24, 1910	November 26 (Mat.) 1910
Klytemnestra	Bahr-Mildenburg	Bahr-Mildenburg	Goetz
Orestes	Austin	Austin	Austin
Aegisthus	D'Oisly	D'Oisly	D'Oisly
Conductor	Beecham	Beecham	Beecham

Designer and Stage Manager not stated.

Despite excellent casting, singing and performances, *Elektra* revived was not the enormous success it had been at the beginning of the year and attendances fell off progressively. The first two performances saw familiar singers in the parts, and of Edyth Walker *The Times* said 'those who have heard her often in the part have never heard her sing it better. Her *mezzo-voce* was exquisite in its quality, she never shouted, even in the loudest passages, and her acting was as imaginative and vigorous as ever. She had excellent support in the Chrysothemis of Frau Petzl-Perard who has a firm, clear voice and knows how to subordinate herself as Chrysothemis without dropping out of the picture. As Klytemnestra, Frau Mildenburg repeated a performance which has made her famous all over the world.'

The Times mused on the possibility of hearing *Salome*, since the ban on it had now been lifted; and also *Guntram*, 'down on the list for future productions[1] . . . Even without *Salome* London will be able to judge of the strides that Strauss has taken since the days of his youth. The stride is much longer between *Guntram* and *Feuersnot* than between *Feuersnot* and *Salome* or *Elektra* (these two may be considered as belonging to the same period) . . .'

At the last performance on November 26—a special matinée—*The Times* urged its readers to remember that 'Londoners are apt to underestimate the great value of operatic matinées to those who are unable to remain to the end of late evening performances'.

The fourth interpreter of Elektra for the last two performances was Mme. Thila Plaichinger. 'She was very striking. . . . What pathos there is in it she fully realises and while keeping the mania of the character well in view, she imparts to it something of the large dignity that some people are still fond of connecting with Greek tragedy. Her voice, too, was in fine order . . . her dance at the end was fittingly grotesque and insane. The curious scene of invective with Klytemnestra was rather more credibly arranged than at first, for Elektra mounted the two steps of the altar and stood over her mother so as to terrify her, in a way that was not done at the first production here' (*The Times*).

Fräulein Marie Goetz, the new Klytemnestra, could not efface the memory of Frau Mildenburg but 'the grimace with which she left the stage reminded the spectator of some conventional tragic mask' (*The Times*).

Frederic Austin was described, as before, as a 'dignified and impressive Orestes' (*The Times*).

---

[1] *Guntram* has never been produced in Britain.

Elektra on Provincial Tour 1912
The Denhof Grand Opera Company Festival Performances

Ernst Denhof was a German-Swiss who lived in Edinburgh between 1896 and 1913 and described himself as a music teacher. He had toured opera with success (and local financial support) in the German States, and in 1911 visited Leeds, Manchester and Glasgow. The success of this tour prompted him to plan a longer one for 1912 and, in addition, to gain the support of Mr. Beecham so as to secure the rights of performing Strauss' *Elektra* for the first time in English to provincial audiences. Both these he did.

Hull obtained 'the honour of having performed in its Grand Theatre the first English language as well as the first provincial performance . . .' of the work. The *Hull Daily Mail* calculated that '. . . in this week or next, preparatory to Herr Denhof's majestic enterprise . . . 50 rehearsals will be held in Hull'. The conductor of *Elektra* was Herr (Hof-Kapell-meister) Fritz Cortolezis of Munich. He had rehearsed the first production of *Der Rosen-kavalier* in Dresden and was brought to England by Beecham with Strauss's blessing.

Grand Theatre, Hull
February 29, March 2 (*mat.*), 1912. World première in English

Elektra	Easton
Chrysothemis	Edith Evans
Klytemnestra	Woodall
Orestes	Austin
Aegisthus	D'Oisly
Conductor	Cortolezis

The première was well received. 'Herr Cortolezis was sitting where, tower-like, he presided over that glowing pit of sound, vulcan-like' (*Hull Daily Mail*). This paper did not much care, however, for the decadent version of the ultra-modern and extremely Teutonic Hugo von Hofmannsthal, but felt that what could be considered a debased account of the Sophocles drama had been enriched, if not saved, by the 'original and magic web of sound' woven by Strauss. The Hull audience, 'which had been in unrelaxed, nervous tension for two hours', was 'large, surprised and enthusiastic'. All the singers, it was reported, 'were competent'.

Theatre Royal, Manchester

	March 7, 1912	March 9, 1912
Elektra	Easton	Gleeson-White
Chrysothemis	Edith Evans	Edith Evans
Klytemnestra	Brema	Woodall
Orestes	Austin	Austin
Aegisthus	D'Oisly	D'Oisly
Conductor	Cortolezis	Cortolezis

Shakespeare Theatre, Liverpool
March 11, 13, 1912

Elektra	Easton
Chrysothemis	Edith Evans
Klytemnestra	Brema
Orestes	Austin
Aegisthus	D'Oisly
Conductor	Cortolezis

The *Liverpool Post* reported that '. . . the outcome was comparative clearness . . . and was due very largely to the discretion of Herr Fritz Cortolezis, a constant companion of Strauss...' As Klytemnestra 'Marie Brema was sublime. . . . Seizing a wand, she moved in agitated trepidation through the ranks of the others, leaning on the support . . . and delivering with awe-inspiring verve, the long drawn-out curse'.

Theatre Royal, Leeds

	March 21, 1912	*March 23 (Mat.), 1912*
Elektra	Easton	Gleeson-White
Chrysothemis	Edith Evans	Edith Evans
Klytemnestra	Brema	Woodall
Orestes	Austin	Austin
Aegisthus	D'Oisly	D'Oisly
Conductor	Cortolezis	Cortolezis

Theatre Royal, Glasgow
March 26, 1912. Scottish première of *Electra*★

Electra★	Easton
Chrysothemis	Edith Evans
Klytemnestra	Brema
Orestes	Austin
Aegisthus	D'Oisly
Conductor	Cortolezis

★ Thus spelt in the Glasgow programme and Press.

Royal Opera House, Covent Garden
Third Beecham Opera Season 1913
February 7, 1910, for three performances in German

	February 7, 10, 1913	*February 13 (Mat.) 1913*
Elektra	Fassbender	Fassbender
Chrysothemis	Petzl-Perard	Petzl-Perard
Klytemnestra	Bahr-Mildenburg	Bahr-Mildenburg

	February 7, 10, 1913	*February* 13 (Mat.), 1913
Orestes	Brodersen	Pacyna
Aegisthus	Bardsley	Bardsley
Conductor	Beecham	Beecham

Costumes by Fisher Ltd.   Stage Manager: Hermann Gura

During 1912 Beecham was busy conducting in England, championing Delius both here and in Germany (where he and his orchestra appeared in Berlin), and carefully watching 'the monumental failure of Mr. Hammerstein and his new opera house'.[1]

Beecham's new season in the winter of early 1913 included three Strauss operas: *Rosenkavalier*, *Elektra* and *Salome*. Perhaps the impact of the first and the still novel *Salome* were responsible for pushing *Elektra* into the shade. Attendances were not good and Beecham, as conductor, was criticised for not husbanding his musical resources. 'Time after time he forestalled the real climaxes' (*The Times*).

The *Illustrated London News* found that the opera was this time revived 'without the old thrill. There was no light and shade, and the light was only expressed by the music in terms of its beauty'.

Elektra passed out of public favour in London after these three performances, and with very infrequent revivals did not return to its former success until 1957.

The Denhof Grand Opera Company
Provincial Tour, 1913

Mr. Ernst Denhof planned another tour of opera in English, this time for fourteen weeks in the autumn of 1913, to six main provincial cities in England and to three in Scotland. One newspaper (unidentified) stated 'only Mr. Denhof could imagine a scheme so courageous as that of his proposed raid of the provinces. . . . Ambition has seldom, in operative affairs in England, flown so high.' The Company consisted of twenty-seven principal singers, a chorus of one hundred, a Ballet of twenty-four and eighty-two in the orchestra. Mr. Thomas Beecham was to be the principal conductor, assisted by Mr. Schilling-Ziemssen. *Elektra* and *Rosenkavalier* were in the repertoire.

Prince of Wales Theatre, Birmingham
September 16, 1913

Theatre Royal, Manchester
October 3, 1913

Elektra	Gleeson-White
Chrysothemis	Edith Evans
Klytemnestra	Brema
Orestes	Austin
Aegisthus	de Sousa
Conductor	Schilling-Ziemssen

[1] *Beecham*, p. 112.

26

At the end of the third week of the tour the Denhof Opera Company had lost £4,000 and the singers and musicians feared—although nothing had been officially said—that they might all face financial disaster on the Saturday evening. So on the Thursday a 'serious and responsible' member of the Company[1] got in touch with Beecham (who was in London) and he replied by telegram to Denhof on the Saturday: 'Endeavour keep Company quiet. Arrive 8.40.' This he did—during the evening performance of *The Flying Dutchman*, after which Denhof did not appear when called.

Thomas Beecham addressed the cast upon the stage, after the last curtain had fallen, and said:

'Ladies and gentlemen, hitherto I have appeared before you and have been known to you as an artist, as you all are. And as an artist I have every sympathy with Mr. Denhof and yourselves; so if it is possible I shall step into the breach and be of assistance. (Cheers.) Quiet. I have come down from London at great inconvenience and I have just a minute. I must have quiet. I am prepared to carry on this season from Sheffield. Nothing possibly can be done this week. The theatre here is let. If I can have the other theatres this tour will be continued till the end of the fortnight in Edinburgh at least. We shall all be able to let you know what future is in store by Wednesday morning at latest. Good night.' (Cheers.)

Several of the principals had offered to give up their salaries to pay the chorus, but these were paid in full up to Saturday, and the orchestra were paid 30 per cent of theirs. A Mr. John Hart and United Theatres Company helped financially.

On the same day the *Daily Sketch* said: 'The Denhof Grand Opera Company, the biggest and finest Company ever sent round the provinces, closed down at Manchester on Saturday night [October 4] . . . In rehearsing the Denhof Company, Mr. Beecham spared no pains to be able to present a performance which should be equal to Covent Garden productions. The poor support from the public was a great disappointment to Mr. Thomas Beecham, who has long cherished the ideal that grand opera on a large scale could be made to pay in the provinces.' Mr. Denhof said: 'There is not much to say. . . . The people of Manchester have not supported us, so it is not possible to go on. After the tremendous success of former years here they take no notice, in spite of the support which the Press had given. . . .'

In his autobiography, *A Mingled Chime*, Sir Thomas has a few interesting points to make about this tour. One shows his method of working and the other reveals that up to this time it had not been considered proper to promote by editorial publicity the theatre in the provinces. On his arrival in Manchester ('which at that time looked upon itself as the true musical capital of England') he found 'a pretty state of things. . . . The audiences . . . had proved unexpectedly meagre . . . the prospects elsewhere were not rosy, the impresario's resources had dried up, and the company, perhaps the largest ever sent on the road, was facing the unpleasant possibility of being thrown out of work for ten or eleven weeks. Was there anything that I could do about it? I called in a brace of auditors, procured the seating plans of all the theatres due to be visited, worked the telephone line in a score of directions, and after twenty-four hours discovered that if we could sell out every single seat

[1] *Beecham*, p. 122.

for each remaining performance during the rest of the tour, we had a sporting chance of getting through fairly well after all. How could this be done? Only through a hurricane campaign of publicity that would reach and wake up even the most lethargic and indifferent creature who had ever heard of the terms *music* and *opera*. But clearly there was no time to launch the kind of effort I had in mind over the weekend for the remaining portion of the Manchester visit. . . .

'About ten days later we reopened the tour in Sheffield. To me at the time the most noteworthy feature of this episode was the first use on a large scale of a method of public propaganda which I have found invaluable on numerous subsequent occasions. . . . I must do full justice to the Press for the handsomest co-operation conceivable, for they gave me almost unlimited space for a series of philippics upon the whole duty of society to art and the artist.

'The first reaction on the part of those attacked and admonished was a fit of sudden fury . . . the next was a rush to the box office . . . and the result was that by the time I arrived to conduct the opening performance, the first week in Sheffield was almost sold out. Upon my appearance in the orchestral pit the house maintained a profound and deadly silence; but at the conclusion . . . I was greeted with a shout, "Well, Tommy Beecham, are we musical?"'

At Leeds, Liverpool and on a return visit to Manchester, there were no performances of *Elektra*.

Theatre Royal, Newcastle upon Tyne
November 13, 1913, in English

King's Theatre, Edinburgh
November 21, 1913, in English

Elektra	Gleeson-White
Chrysothemis	Edith Evans
Klytemnestra	Terry
Orestes	Austin
Aegisthus	de Sousa
Conductor	Schilling-Ziemssen

The *Scotsman* said *Elektra* was '. . . performed with more marked impressiveness than at the two previous productions in Scotland . . .' Actually there had been only one.

Thomas Beecham had kept his promise of October 4 to the Company, on which date the tour ended in Edinburgh (ironically the home of Mr. Denhof, who was never in evidence again, but who lived on until 1936). Two dates arranged in the early stages before the tour started, in Aberdeen and Glasgow, were cancelled.

So ended the Denhof Opera Company *per se*. It was now virtually to pass to the control of Thomas Beecham who, despite many vicissitudes, went on conducting, producing and financing opera in England up to 1955.

Royal Opera House, Covent Garden

Grand Opera Season 1925

May 26, 1925, for two performances

	May 26, 1925	June 1, 1925
Elektra	Kappel	Kappel
Chrysothemis	Landwehr	Landwehr
Klytemnestra	Olczewska	Olczewska
Orestes	Schorr	Schorr
Aegisthus	Soot	Soot
Conductor	Walter	Heger

Designer not stated   The Stage under the direction of Charles Moor

This unappreciated revival included new scenery and a German and Austrian cast, all entirely familiar with their roles yet never before heard in them here. *The Times* said, '*Elektra* was due for revival. It was a dozen years or so since it was last heard at Covent Garden; it may be a dozen years, more or less, before it is heard again, for there is not the least prospect of its passing into the popular repertory in this country. But it is certain that it will recur from time to time when there is a German company here capable of giving it as it was given under Herr Bruno Walter's direction last night.'

Gertrud Kappel's Elektra did not have a sufficiently 'commanding presence. . . . Whenever we could hear her she was singing with all her usual truth and purity of style, but she never seemed to fulfil the description of her . . . as a wild and savage creature. Mme. Olczewska's presentation of Klytemnestra is repulsive enough to satisfy even von Hofmannsthal's loathsome conception of the character,[1] though it must be confessed that her grotesque make-up when she first appeared at the window brought to the irreverent mind the suggestion of a figure in a Punch and Judy show. It was an example of the way the over-insistence on physical characteristics may defeat the purposes of tragedy'[2] (*The Times*).

Both Rose Landwehr and Friedrich Schorr as Chrysothemis and Orestes were highly satisfactory, especially Schorr, whose voice brought 'a splendid relief into this orgy of screaming sopranos' (*The Times*).

The production came seriously under fire for appallingly bad lighting (which reads like a notice of 1948–52), but worse, for allowing the murder of Aegisthus to be seen: quite contrary to the stage directions in the score.[3]

[1] 'She is so horrible a spectacle that the Greek imagination, surely, would have shunned from it. Sleepless nights, remorse, haunting fears, have undermined her. Her sallow, bloated face shows up in the lurid light of the torches against her scarlet robe. Her eyelids are unnaturally large, and she seems to hold them open with difficulty. She is covered with jewels, rings, armlets, all of them talismans against evil. She leans heavily on her confidante, whose dark violet robe contrasts sombrely with hers, and on an ivory staff set with gems' (Ernest Newman, *Opera Nights*, 1943, p. 152).

[2] See *Salome* 1949.

[3] In a letter to von Hofmannsthal, Strauss wrote (December 22, 1907): 'As for our recent conversation about *Elektra*, I believe that we can't leave out Aegisthus altogether. He is definitely part of the plot and must be killed with the rest, preferably before the eyes of the audience' (*Correspondence*, p. 12). But von Hofmannsthal did not like this, so evidently the final result of Aegisthus seen dying, from one window to another as he moves inside the palace, was a form of compromise.

With such a cast and under such noble direction, this was a revival which merited better support and greater appreciation. The opera was preceded by 'Strauss's tone-poem *Tod und Verklärung* also under Herr Walter's masterful baton' (*The Times*).

At the second performance, with an identical cast, Robert Heger, from Munich, conducted.

Royal Opera House, Covent Garden
Beecham Grand Opera Season 1938
May 5, 9, 1938 for two performances in German

Elektra	Pauly
Chrysothemis	H. Konetzni
Klytemnestra	Thorborg
Orestes	Janssen
Aegisthus	Wolff
Conductor	Beecham

Scenery by Aravantinos   Producer: Charles Moor

Beecham conducting *Elektra* again at Covent Garden—after twenty-five years! The cast was of a third generation of Strauss singers, with Rose Pauly as 'an artist who realizes the character completely in voice and action' (*The Times*). She was a famous interpreter of the part in Europe and America, and this revival, according to Ernest Newman, was one in a lifetime.

'Mme. Kerstin Thorborg presented a striking figure of the debased and distraught Klytemnestra. Her singing equalled her acting in the part, and Herr Janssen who, as Orestes, has only one short dialogue with Elektra . . . made the right impression by his unaffected and dignified singing of it' (*The Times*).

As 'the ingenuous Chrysothemis' Mme. Hilde Konetzni, perhaps because her make-up and costume were out of keeping, was unable to make the character appealing—despite some admirable singing.

The sets were borrowed from the Staatsoper, Berlin, and were considered to be underlit. Sir Thomas Beecham was again criticised by *The Times* for blurring his dramatic situations, although his mastery of the score was not denied.

Royal Opera House, Covent Garden
1952/53 Season
May 13, 1953, for four performances in German

	May 13, 1953	*May 15, 1953*	*May 23, 27, 1953*
Elektra	Schlüter	Schlüter	Schlüter
Chrysothemis	Kupper	Kinasiewitz	Kupper
Klytemnestra	Coates	Coates	Coates
Orestes	Braun	Braun	Braun

	May 13, 1953	May 15, 1953	May 23, 27, 1953
Aegisthus	Edgar Evans	Edgar Evans	Edgar Evans
Conductor	Kleiber	Kleiber	Kleiber

Scenery and Costumes by Isabel Lambert★   Producer: Rudolf Hartmann

★ The widow of Constant Lambert.

Eric Blom in the *Observer* records that 'the repertory of the Royal Opera House has been enriched by a new production of Strauss's *Elektra*, and few things, if any, are better done at Covent Garden. . . . We are really back in the grand international seasons and . . . this work is not only given in German with German principals, but conducted by Erich Kleiber and produced by Rudolf Hartmann. Isabel Lambert's impressive setting of the palace at Mycenae dominated the production, a grey-black courtyard that enclosed the players like a monstrous cage.' 'It had little but good detail, such as the huge bronze doors with enormous ring knockers in the centre' (*The Times*).

'The outstanding feature of [the] production was Erich Kleiber's superb handling of the orchestral score' (*Sunday Times*) and 'those richest pages of the score found the orchestra, after a taxing hour and a half, ready to play with a splendour of tone that feasted the ear' (*The Times*).

The central figure, Elektra, was Erna Schlüter, who had frequently sung the part in Hamburg and once over the BBC under Beecham in 1947. *The Times* described her as 'large of physique, sometimes unsteady of voice at the top of the treble stave but an artist of such vivid power and such integrity that her characterisation brushed aside all imperfections'.

'The first sight of her was gruesome enough but in the recognition scene her face and her carriage took on a look of noble and moving beauty, and her expression of joy when she moved towards Orestes, crying his name, was like a shaft of blinding sunlight . . .' (William Mann in *Opera*).

In three out of the four performances, Annelies Kupper sang Chrysothemis but she 'remained commonplace dramatically' (*Observer*). Hans Braun sang Orestes 'with a splendid voice, obvious intelligence and a fine presence' (*Observer*). As Klytemnestra, Edith Coates's interpretation was not considered to be in the right key, yet, as always, this artist gave a complete and striking performance. Edgar Evans, in the brief part of Aegisthus, was variously described as looking 'like an M.P. after a trying day in the House', 'as if he had strayed out of the chorus of *Iolanthe*', and 'Disraeli to the life'.

On the second night of the revival (May 15) Maria Kinasiewitz sang Chrysothemis in a voice too hard for the character. Her acting followed this pattern.

Royal Opera House, Covent Garden
1953/54 Season
April 30, 1954, for three performances in German

	April 30, May 4, 1954	May 7, 1954
Elektra	Schlüter	Schlüter
Chrysothemis	Rysanek	Rysanek

	April 30, May 4, 1954	May 7, 1954
Klytemnestra	Coates	Coates
Orestes	O. Kraus	O. Kraus
Aegisthus	Edgar Evans	Nilsson
Conductor	Kempe	Kempe

Scenery by Isabel Lambert   Producer: Rudolf Hartmann

This was a revival of the previous season's production, with the same Elektra, who 'again gave us an impersonation of the bitter heroine which is surely unrivalled today' (*Opera*).[1] There was a golden voiced Chrysothemis in Leonie Rysanek, who gave the character its full meaning and sympathy, as well as a new Orestes in Otakar Kraus, about whom opinions were divided. Edith Coates had modified the fussiness of her previous portrayal of the Queen.

But 'Rudolf Kempe, whose acquaintance London first made during last September's visit of the Bavarian State Opera, conducted so compellingly that some of us were tempted to wonder whether after all Erich Kleiber had said the last word about this Strauss score' (*Opera*).[2]

Royal Festival Hall, London, 1955
Visit of Stuttgart State Opera 1955
September 13, 17, for two performances in German

Elektra	Borkh
Chrysothemis	Kinas
Klytemnestra	Fischer
Orestes	A. Welitsch
Aegisthus	Windgassen
Conductor	Leitner

Scenery and Costumes by Gerd Richter   Producer: Kurt Puhlmann

The only possible reason for trying to convert Festival Hall into an opera house must lie in the large number of seats and the consequent ability to make opera pay there. But if this is so, *Elektra* was a good choice for two reasons. First, it had only received twenty-seven London performances in over forty-four years, because it was not considered 'good box-office' after the first season; and secondly, the action of *Elektra* was suited to the shallow acting area of the make-shift concert platform-cum-stage on the South Bank. But the proscenium is also low, and there was no way of creating any impressiveness or towering height of the palace. Altogether the Covent Garden productions under Kleiber in 1953 and under Kempe in 1954, were much more satisfactory, visually and vocally.

[1] Vol. V, No. 6, p. 376.
[2] *Ibid.*

32

The parts of the two sisters, Elektra and Chrysothemis, might easily have been reversed by Inge Borkh and Maria Kinas[1]; Miss Borkh with the light voice, long blond wig, clean appearance and carefully placed profile was oddly presented. Miss Kinas, on the other hand, had a large voice and looked unkempt and wild. Harold Rosenthal stated in *Opera*, 'I doubt, however, whether the music has ever been sung with such accuracy. But I would rather put up with the inaccuracies and even the inability to sing some of the notes and have a Rose Pauly or an Erna Schlüter.'

As Klytemnestra, Res Fischer was said to have sung it better a few years previously, yet she gave 'a fine, authoritative study of the haunted, malign queen' (*The Times*). 'The other parts went for hardly anything and were much better done at Covent Garden' (*Opera*).

The orchestral playing, after the sublime performances at Covent Garden, seemed dull and was 'often inaccurate' (*Opera*) under Dr. Leitner, and the musicians suffered a disadvantage, both acoustically as well as physically, by having to play in an improvised pit which was no pit at all.

This revival was a welcome opportunity to hear Stuttgart's unfamiliar voices in the opera, but coming, as it did, between two such important Covent Garden productions, it paled by comparison.

The other works in the repertory of the Stuttgart State Opera on this visit were *Tristan und Isolde*, *Die Zauberflote*, and Wieland Wagner's realisation of *Fidelio*, by far the most interesting and controversial of the four.

Royal Opera House, Covent Garden
1957/58 Season
November 16, 19, 22, 27, 1957, for four performances in German

Elektra	Lammers
Chrysothemis	Müller-Bütow
Klytemnestra	von Milinkovič
Orestes	O. Kraus
Aegisthus	Edgar Evans
Conductor	Kempe

Scenery and Costumes by Isabel Lambert   Producer not stated

Christel Goltz—heard in London as Salome, but never as Elektra—had been advertised to sing in this revival of the opera; the young Norwegian soprano, Aase Nordmo Lovberg, was to be the Chrysothemis. In the event neither appeared. The three current Elektras—Birgit Nilsson, Varnay and Borkh—were not available. The management of the Opera House tried to find a fourth—Gerda Lammers—of whom Lord Harewood had heard.[2] After much telephoning round Germany, she was found rehearsing for a recital in—of all places—one of the smallest concert halls in London. Gerda Lammers was quickly taken to

[1] Formerly known as Kinasiewitz, this Polish soprano had sung Chrysoltemis at Covent Garden in May 1953.
[2] Gerda Lammers had been a leading German concert singer before making her operatic début at Kassel in 1955.

the stage of Covent Garden where, after only fifteen minutes, she convinced those who were listening to her that she was an outstanding Elektra.

And so it was proved. Lammers was a superb actress as well as a great singer, and her first performance was one of those rare events in the opera house when a new star unexpectedly emerges. Ernest Newman said in the *Sunday Times*: 'Her voice proved itself one of commanding power, dramatically the right thing for Elektra, yet always gratifyingly musical and always dead in tune, while towards the end of the exacting work, after all the strain of the opening and middle portions of the drama, her voice was extraordinarily appealing by the tender beauty of its timbre in the more relaxed portions of the great "recognition" scene.'

Hedwig Müller-Bütow, from Berlin, was the Chrysothemis, but beside Lammers she seemed to have 'no more than everyday accomplishment' (*Opera*); and Georgine von Milinkovič as Klytemnestra was presented 'with vivid dramatic characterization—one could feel the beat of the wings of the Erinyes about her painted face and above the hollow tones of her fevered voice' (*The Times*).

Orestes and the smaller parts were in most capable hands. Kempe was criticised for not letting the orchestra 'go' enough (no doubt he was carefully nursing Lammers along) and William Mann in *Opera* missed a certain savagery which was lost 'in favour of structural clarity'.

Royal Opera House, Covent Garden
1957/58 Season
May 14, 1958, for four performances in German

	May 14, 16, 1958	*May 29, 31, 1958*
Elektra	Lammers	Lammers
Chrysothemis	Schech	Müller-Bütow
Klytemnestra	von Milinkovič	von Milinkovič
Orestes	O. Kraus	O. Kraus
Aegisthus	Edgar Evans	Edgar Evans
Conductor	Kempe	Kempe

Scenery and Costumes by Isabel Lambert   Producer not stated

The only newcomer in this revival was Marianne Schech, who sang Chrysothemis, but unexceptionally. *The Times* said that Lammers sung her music 'with a clean, beautiful tone worthy of Mozart, and an intellectual acumen more to be associated with Lieder-singing; to these Mme. Lammers adds a histrionic performance of great dignity and expressiveness, simple in resource but infinitely wide in range of human feeling'. The *Observer*, likewise, felt that 'if anything the months . . . have brought a deepened mystery of this prodigiously taxing role. . . . Sheer precision in singing is a far more exciting quality in singing than may at first appear.'

'Otakar Kraus was a moving and dignified Orestes' and 'the orchestra under Kempe was at its best, and the conductor again demonstrated his outstanding gifts as both interpreter and accompanist' (*Opera*).

Royal Opera House, Covent Garden

1959/60 Season
May 30, June 1, 7, 9, 1960, for four performances in German

Elektra	Lammers
Chrysothemis	Kuchta
Klytemnestra	Höngen
Orestes	O. Kraus
Aegisthus	Edgar Evans
Conductor	Kempe

Scenery and Costumes by Isabel Lambert   Production rehearsed by Ande Anderson

Lammers's esteem increased as the season went on. Andrew Porter in *Opera* could not have been more exuberant about her. 'One does not compare an Elektra with a Brünnhilde or Norma . . . to declare this the greatest single performance that post-war Covent Garden has seen may mean little . . . certainly I have seen no other performance where, vocally, interpretatively, dramatically, one could not imagine any phrase being done better. The silences, the whispered utterances, the acting, the way words are pronounced, are as memorable as the great climaxes.'

Elisabeth Höngen was making her first London appearance in the part of Klytemnestra and was 'for the first time at Covent Garden a Klytemnestra to match her daughter. This is no superannuated tart, fallen on hard days, such as we have seen in former years, but the wreck of a vastly formidable and ruthless woman, now in dissolution, yet still imposing and capable of inspiring terror' (*Observer*).

Gladys Kuchta as Chrysothemis had 'a rich, powerful voice, just a little ripe perhaps for the role . . . and Otakar Kraus, though hardly superlative, is a capable Orestes' (*Financial Times*).

'But it is the orchestra which imparts dramatic tension to the characterization provided by the singers. Since Mr. Rudolf Kempe was in charge of it, the long act unrolled from an intense start to an intense finish, but with no anti-climaxes and plenty of rise and fall' (*The Times*).

Summary of Performances

London	41
Hull	2
Manchester	3
Liverpool	2
Leeds	2
Birmingham	1
Newcastle upon Tyne	1
Glasgow	1
Edinburgh	1
TOTAL	54

FEUERSNOT

FEUERSNOT

AFTER THE INDIFFERENT RECEPTION at Weimar in 1894 of *Guntram*, Strauss's first opera, he devoted his energy to the composition of large-scale orchestral works: *Till Eulenspiegel*, *Zarathustra*, and *Don Quixote*. Strauss was then appointed to the post of Königlicher Hof-Kappelmeister in Berlin. After the composition of *Ein Heldenleben* in 1899 during an intense period of conducting, the score of *Feuersnot* was completed on May 22, 1901.

In Strauss's own words '. . . I came across the Flemish legend, *The Quenched Fires of Audenarde*, which gave me the idea of writing, with personal motives, a little *intermezzo* against the theatre, to wreak some vengeance on my dear native town where I, little Richard the Third (there is no 'second', Hans von Bülow once said) just like the great Richard the First thirty years before, had such unpleasant experiences'. Strauss wrote these words in the form of a reminiscence some forty years later;[1] and referred of course, to Wagner's expulsion from Munich by his enemies, despite the patronage of King Ludwig II of Bavaria.

Feuersnot (called *Les Feux de la Sainte Jean* in French, and either *Fire Famine* or *Beltane Fire* in English) has a libretto by Ernst von Wolzogen, who later tried unsuccessfully to interest Strauss in further collaboration.

Feuersnot may be considered not only an 'intermezzo' as Strauss put it, but also a transitional move towards the first, original style of *Salome* and *Elektra*.

Thomas Beecham, with a touch of flippancy, said of the opera 'The chief features of this gay and audacious work are the number and difficulty of the choruses and the indelicacy of the story. . . . The hero, who has most of the serious stuff to sing, is a hero of the first order, but the other characters are attractively and amusingly drawn. . . .'[2] The note on the opera in the Fifth Edition of Grove is far more complimentary when it states that *Feuersnot* gives '. . . full scope for brilliantly effective treatment of the folksong elements of music, for musical sarcasm and for voluptuous love music. The finale is one of the most gorgeously coloured of his [Strauss's] tone pictures and the choruses are remarkable for almost unsuspected powers of solid choral architecture.'

Feuersnot has never been revived in Britain since 1910 when it was given in the Thomas Beecham Season of *opéra comique* together with *Tales of Hoffmann*, *Werther*, *Fledermaus* and *Nozze di Figaro*.

[1] *Recollections*, p. 149.
[2] *Beecham*, p. 96.

The Story of the Opera

The curtain rises on a square in Munich in the twelfth century as the townsfolk are about to celebrate the festival of Midsummer, St. John the Baptist's Eve, by burning bonfires. The children are collecting wood and they demand tribute from the Burgomaster's house. Here they are graciously received. He has a big bundle of faggots for them, and his daughter Diemut and her three playmates, Margret, Elsbeth and Wigelis, come from the house and distribute sweets amongst the children. Presently they hammer at the door of a house opposite the Burgomaster's, inhabited by Kunrad, believed to be an alchemist, who presently appears.

Kunrad is young, and is struck by the gaiety of the children, and still more by the beauty of the Burgomaster's daughter, Diemut. He gives the children permission to seize all they can find for their bonfire. Considerable hubbub ensues and Kunrad declares that henceforth he will devote himself to 'reading in Nature's book'. He suddenly makes a leap at Diemut and kisses her right on the lips. This act is succeeded by a general outcry, but the festival must not be interrupted, and dancing is commenced to the strains of a waltz.

While this has been going on, the shades of evening have been falling. The bailiff of the town enters and tries to placate Diemut, but she is very angry and exclaims, 'Sir, I have not a word to say', and retires. Kunrad comforts himself by singing an impassioned love-song, which convinces the bailiff that he has gone mad. Left alone, Kunrad watches his beloved's window, and presently is rewarded by seeing her on the balcony combing her hair. The result is a duet, in which it appears she would not have been so angry with Kunrad had not the townsfolk seen him kiss her. But she means to have her revenge.

She leads Kunrad on to think she has forgiven him, and induces him to enter the firewood basket on the pretence she will hoist him to her balcony, but she leaves him hanging half-way up and calls her friends. The inhabitants assemble and jeer Kunrad; but they are awed to silence when he weaves a spell which puts out all the lights in the town. There is another uproar, and the townspeople threaten Kunrad with dire penalties as soon as he descends to earth.

But Kunrad is master of the situation, and takes the opportunity of haranguing them at length on failing to recognise the geniuses who have dwelt among them. At the end of his speech Kunrad declares that 'Alone through womanly passion once more the fire for you shall glow.'

The stage has now become quite dark. The people comment on Kunrad's speech, and call on Diemut to 'kiss and be quits'. Presently Diemut appears on the balcony and takes Kunrad into her room. Then the orchestra commences a significant interlude, concerning which it may be said with the townsfolk 'Honi soit qui mal y pense'. As the strains proceed they become increasingly impassioned and finally work up to a tremendous climax when, to quote the stage directions, 'The lights in the house, and torches, etc., burst forth into flame simultaneously'. The people shout for joy and Kunrad and Diemut are heard singing

> Midsummer night!
> Heart's deep desire!
> Ah, that it might never end!

(*There was no synopsis in the Programme. The above is taken from a contemporary account.*)

40

His Majesty's Theatre, London

The Thomas Beecham Opéra Comique Season 1910
July 9, 1910 (British première) for five performances in English

	July 9, 13, 1910	July 11, 1910	July 15,* 22, 1910
Burgomaster	Radford	Radford	Radford
Kunrad	Oster	Austin	Austin
Diemut	Fay	Fay	Edith Evans
Elsbeth	Maitland	Maitland	Maitland
Wigelis	Phelps	Phelps	Phelps
Margret	Coomber	Coomber	Coomber
Conductor	Beecham	Beecham	Beecham

Designer not stated   Producer: Louis Verande

* Followed by Act II of *Tales of Hoffmann* (Venetian Scene).

The general public did not respond very favourably to this particular opera during the season—in some quarters on moral grounds—but mainly because of the increased prices asked for admission.[1] The *Daily Telegraph* complained that 'the whole spirit of the original work reeks of the Sentlingerstrasse, Munich, and can but transfer badly to the Haymarket, London, where the point is apt to be missed in so many local songs and allusions, in their unblushing impurity'.

The work—unusually for Mr. Beecham—was said to be under-rehearsed, but improved greatly as the cast became more confident. In an effort to bring in better audiences, the second act of *Hoffmann* was given as well at the fourth performance. Writing many years later of *Feuersnot*, Beecham said: 'Those who saw the piece fully shared my partiality for it, but the larger public could not be induced to patronize it. . . .'[2]

Beecham's enterprise and his handling of the orchestra received just praise, as did the 'extremely clever translation' of William Wallace,[3] 'whose easy familiarity with nearly every known art and craft had long marked him out as one of the most versatile characters of the day'.[4]

Doubt was expressed at the need to employ foreign artists for the two leading roles, but this was done because Oster and Fay had frequently played the parts before. The difficult chorus work—often sung in a multiplicity of keys simultaneously—called for precise intonation from all concerned, and often this was not forthcoming.

The Times critic returned to the third performance and pointed out that 'Strauss went

[1] Boxes 6 gns., instead of 4 gns.; Stalls 21s. instead of 10s. 6d.; Upper Circle 7s. 6d. instead of 5s. and the Gallery raised from 1s. 6d. to 2s. 6d.

[2] *Beecham*, p. 96.

[3] Not to be confused with the composer of *Maritana*, Wallace (1860–1940) was a medical graduate, composer, musicologist and water-colourist.

[4] *Beecham*, p. 75.

out of his way to proclaim it as a second *Meistersinger* and that is a position he has been quite unable to maintain. Judged merely as a comic opera of a rather slender kind it has a great many excellent features . . . but whenever Kunrad is on the stage the composer seems beset with his determination to make the part impressive and consequently it becomes very dull.' As a whole this critic felt it was 'an admirably spirited performance' in which Mr. Beecham 'achieved a remarkable feat in making the children sing their difficult music so accurately'.

The *Illustrated London News* critic stated that 'the story is offensive and the music poor . . . and it is an open question whether Strauss's latter-day genius can make this early work acceptable or gain for it in England anything more than a very brief hearing'. The end of this statement has been borne out by history, but Strauss and von Hofmannsthal were at that moment in time polishing the almost complete *Der Rosenkavalier*, and had reached a mature creative unison.

Strauss himself had still got thirty-four years of composition ahead. It would seem that the imputation of 'latter-day' genius was somewhat wide of the mark.

Summary of Performances

London   .   .   .   .   TOTAL   5

SALOME

SALOME

ACCORDING TO STRAUSS,[1] he met a friend after seeing a performance of Wilde's play *Salome* in Berlin. The friend, Heinrich Grunfeld, said: 'My dear Strauss, surely you could make an opera of this!' He replied, 'I am busy composing it already.' The Viennese poet, Anton Lindtner, said Strauss, sent 'cleverly versified opening scenes, but I could not make up my mind to start composing until one day it occurred to me to set to music *Wie schön ist die Prinzessin Salome heute Nacht* straight away'. And this, of course, is how the opera starts, with just enough orchestra to bring up a quick curtain before Narraboth plunges in to the heart of the action.

The opera was produced in Dresden on December 9, 1905. The critics gave it little chance of success. 'Three weeks later it had, I think, been accepted by ten theatres,' Strauss says.[1]

After one performance at the Metropolitan Opera House, New York, in 1906, the opera was taken out of the repertoire and the Board declared the work 'objectionable' and 'operatic offal'. But the outcry soon died down, apart from another in Vienna led by a certain 'prelate rejoicing in the perhaps not altogether inapposite name of Piffl'.[2]

But it was with the royalties from *Salome* that Strauss was able to build his villa in Garmisch, where he lived and composed for the rest of his life.

For his second Covent Garden season Beecham continued to pursue a policy of presenting unknown operas with the familiar, and after the success of *Elektra* he decided to produce *Salome*. He cast a Finnish soprano, Aïno Ackté, in the leading part, 'a slim and beautiful creature with an adequate voice and a remarkable understanding of her part'.[3] As soon as Beecham's intentions became known the Lord Chamberlain advised him that he would be refused a licence for performance.

Beecham sought the private ear of the Prime Minister, Mr. Asquith, pointing out that 'Strauss was the most famous and in common opinion the greatest of living composers; this was his most popular work; it was to be played . . . to those who wanted to hear it; it did not concern . . . those that did not want to hear it; being given in German it would be comprehended by few; and lastly . . . we might run the risk of making ourselves slightly ridiculous in the eyes of the rest of the world by taking an exceptional attitude towards a celebrated work of art, as we had done so often in the past before the advent to power of the present enlightened Government.'

[1] *Recollections*, pp. 150–152.
[2] Ernest Newman: *Sunday Times*.
[3] *Beecham*, p. 97 ff.

Some weeks later Beecham was invited to attend the Lord Chamberlain, who said that he thought he had found a way out. 'If you will consent to certain modifications of the text likely to disarm the scruples of the devout it will help us to reconsider our decision,' he said. The main cause of censorship lay in the fact that the story of Salome comes from the *New Testament*.

At an early date there was a conference and, after eliminating the name of John, Beecham recalls 'we went on to deprive every passage between him and Salome of the slightest force or meaning. . . . The day arrived when our aim was accomplished and we had successfully metamorphosed a lurid tale of love and revenge into a comforting sermon. . . . I handed over the strange document to my friend Alfred Kalisch, who was to make an equivalently innocuous German version and send it along to the singers for study. . . .'

Rehearsals had hardly begun when it was remembered that Salome had to handle the decapitated head of John the Baptist on the stage. The alternative suggestion of a blood-stained sword was utterly rejected by Mme. Ackté and the eventual compromise was 'a large platter completely covered with a cloth'. This was referred to as *the dish of blood* and it is difficult to understand why it should be considered less repellent. At all events the text (which remained) when Salome sings 'I must kiss your mouth' and later 'I have kissed your mouth' became absolute nonsense. However, it did not all fall out as planned by the Lord Chamberlain.

Beecham's press department worked overtime in November and early December 1910 and produced nearly a dozen handouts. One of these gives the earliest known précis of the opera in this country. Another, of December 1, 1910, announces: 'Dr. Richard Strauss's London agent wishes it to be known that the composer expresses gratification at the selection of Mme. Aïno Ackté to sing and dance the role of Salome, and in the selection of Herr Ernst Kraus to take the part of Herod.'

On the day booking opened for the first performance, the house was sold out in one hour and twenty minutes. Offers of £5 for one guinea stalls were being made outside the box office but 'few were tempted to part with their tickets even for this amount'.

The Story of the Opera

THE THOMAS BEECHAM OPERA COMPANY
ROYAL OPERA HOUSE COVENT GARDEN, W.C.
RICHARD STRAUSS'S FAMOUS OPERA
'SALOME'
TO BE SUNG IN LONDON

The scene is laid upon a terrace of Herod's palace, where soldiers are keeping watch while the King holds revel within.

Salome, the daughter of Herodias, issues from the banquet-chamber, troubled by Herod's gaze. Presently the voice of Jochanaan (John the Baptist) is heard issuing from the cistern hard by, where the prophet is imprisoned. Salome bids Narraboth, a young Assyrian, bring him forth. Dragged from his living tomb, Jochanaan denounces the wickedness of Herodias, but Salome has no ears for his curses. Fascinated by the strange beauty of the prophet she pours forth her passion in wild accents. Jochanaan repulses her and retreats once more to his place of imprisonment.

Herod and Herodias now come forth from the Banquet, and Herod bids Salome dance. She extorts a promise from him that he will give her whatever she asks even to the half of his kingdom, and dances the dance of the seven veils. The dance over, she demands the head of Jochanaan. Herod pleads with her, but in vain. Then the executioner is sent into the cistern, and shortly afterwards the head of Jochanaan is held aloft by the coloured executioner, who has placed it on a silver shield. At once Salome hurries forward, and seizing the head with both her hands, she passionately kisses its lifeless lips.

Instantly Herod, in wrath and horror, cries to his soldiers: 'Kill this woman.' As the curtain falls she is crushed to death beneath their shields.

> *(Synopsis from Thomas Beecham's Office in a Press Hand-out, November, undated, 1910. No synopsis appeared in the programme at Covent Garden until January 11, 1937.)*

Royal Opera House, Covent Garden
Second Beecham Opera Season 1910
December 8, 1910 (British première) for ten performances in German

	December 8, 10, 14 (*mat.*) 1910	December 12, 1910	December 17, 20, 28 (*mat.*), 29, 1910	December 26, 31, 1910
Narraboth	D'Oisly	D'Oisly	D'Oisly	D'Oisly
Prophet	Whitehill	Whitehill	Whitehill	Whitehill
Salome	Ackté	von Rappe	Ackté	Ackté
Herodes	E. Kraus	E. Kraus	Costa	Brozel
Herodias	Metzger	Metzger	Petzl-Demmer	Petzl-Demmer
Conductor	Beecham	Beecham	Beecham	Beecham

Designer not stated   Stage Manager: Louis Verande

Not since the first performance of *Elektra* had there been such interest and anticipation at the Royal Opera House. Once more shocking and sensational rumours were current and part of the aroused interest was undoubtedly of a morbid nature.

The Censor's last word had been so strict, that the packed audience on the first night found a curious descriptive version of the story accompanying the German words. The Prophet's name had become Mattaniah, the story had been moved to Greece, the Nazarenes were called Kappadocians, and a kind of attempted literary brain-washing was in process in an effort to eliminate any connection with the Scriptures. The singers had learned, on their side, the bowdlerised German version with some unwillingness, but then, during the first performance, to quote Thomas Beecham, '... gradually I sensed by the telepathy which

47

exists between the conductor . . . and the artists . . . a growing restlessness and excitement of which the first exhibition was a slip on the part of Salome, who . . . lapsed into the viciousness of the lawful text'.[1]

Beecham was powerless to do anything but imagine the results of this disaster—he 'recalled an experience of Strauss himself at a rehearsal of the same opera when, out of humour with vocal struggles on the stage he had exhorted the orchestra to more strenuous efforts by calling out that he could still hear his singers'[2]; and Beecham tried to do the same. At the end of the opera when Salome's voice could be clearly heard over a gentle orchestral accompaniment, Beecham knew he must admit defeat. But afterwards, when the Lord Chamberlain and his staff congratulated Beecham on the complete way in which he had met and gratified their wishes, he never knew whether imperfect diction, ignorance of German or straightforward diplomacy in a hopeless situation had saved him.

Despite Beecham's singular discomfort, the performance provoked invariable congratulation from the Press. In *The Nation*, Ernest Newman said, 'The representation of the work was highly successful. It was sumptuously mounted, and all scenic arrangements worked. . . . The Oriental scene in front of Herodes's palace looked charming in the pale moonlight. The lighting was excellent. The moon disappeared when the Prophet died. The group of soldiers, the five learned men, whose clever quarrels over matters of creed sounded very ugly indeed, and the glitter and glare of the Court of Herodes made a picturesque effect. In the great title part Mme. Ackté acted and sang with unflagging spirit and striking characterisation. Her Salome was an imperious princess, a spoilt child, and a woman intoxicated with sensuousness. She often caught the tone which indicates the cruel joy and the pleasure of making sure of a victim. Her voice sounded persuasive, strong and pliable, and she is mistress of the speech-song.' Furthermore, she performed the Dance of the Seven Veils herself, which had seldom been done elsewhere, and thus preserved a most significant piece of realism.

As the Prophet, Clarence Whitehill 'achieved a noble vocal triumph. With superb dignity, and with magnificent roundness of tone he cursed her and advised as well as reviled her daughter' (*Daily News*).

'Herr Kraus and Frau Metzger were well suited in the parts of Herodes and Herodias. They sang expressively and showed the unsympathetic qualities of this pair of decadents without exaggeration' (*Daily Mirror*). 'As the handsome and lovesick captain, Mr. D'Oisly sang and acted well' (*Nation*).

In view of Beecham's self-confessed emotions, it is amusing to read the *Daily Mail*'s comments on the orchestra. They 'played with great sensitiveness and energy, and Mr. Beecham was ever on the alert and inspired his forces to sustained and enthusiastic efforts'.

Comparison with *Elektra* was inevitable and *The Times* said 'With all its faults and its many longueurs there can be no doubt that from the musical point of view *Salome* is greatly preferable to *Elektra*, and occasionally, as in the utterances of the Prophet, there is real dignity

[1] *Beecham*, p. 104.
[2] *Beecham*, pp. 104–5.

and breadth. In the final scene, though it reproduces very closely the mood of Isolde's *Liebestod*, there is a high degree of sincerity and musical beauty.' 'It is a work of immense interest in the composer's development', said the *Telegraph*. 'Whether it is destined to survive or not, whether it is even a milestone in the progress of musical things, is on the knees of the gods.'

Although only two performances of *Salome* had originally been announced, it was evident from the response at the box-office that more would be required. At the fourth representation there was a new Salome in Signe von Rappe. She came especially from Vienna for this performance and was said to succeed best in her long, final scene of 'this bizarre setting of Oscar Wilde's masterly study in erotomania' (*Illustrated London News*).

At the last *Salome* performance of the season on New Year's Eve, the entertainment began 'with a vigorous performance of Strauss's *Ein Heldenleben*. . . . This was followed by the now familiar *Salome* in which Mme. Ackté and Mr. Whitehill repeated their triumphs and were worthily supported by a Herod (Mr. Brozel) who was a very great improvement on his predecessors' (*The Times*).

'The music stands on a higher plane than the book, but the only change in the action is the absence of John the Baptist's head. The passages allotted to Salome's lament are of rare beauty, but while it must be admitted that the music is often sufficiently inspired to throw the glamour of beauty over the sordid story, the success of *Salome* indicates nothing more certainly than the decadence of public taste' (*Illustrated London News*).

'There was some enthusiasm on the fall of the curtain, and amid cheers Mr. Beecham was presented with a laurel wreath at the close of the season, instead of the support which ought to have been given him throughout it' (*The Times*).

Royal Opera House, Covent Garden
Third Beecham Opera Season 1913
February 18, 1913, for four performances in German

	February 18, 25, 1913	*February* 21, 1913	*March* 6 (*mat.*), 1913
Narraboth	Bardsley	Bardsley	Bardsley
Prophet	Weil	Wiedermann	Weil
Salome	Ackté	Ackté	Ackté
Herodes	Costa	Costa	Costa
Herodias	Langendorff	Langendorff	Langendorff
Conductor	Beecham	Beecham	Schilling-Ziemssen

The opera was beautifully staged in this revival, and Ackté was as splendid as before. *The Times* commented on the fact that she had a 'dish filled with something which looked like a rolled up tablecloth . . . with a green lime turned on it'. However unpleasant this looked it was not thought 'as nasty as the more realistic dish of blood of two years ago.'

This paper acknowledged that the responsibility for the makeshift property did not lie with the management.

Beecham was criticised (as he was in the same season's *Elektra*) for being musically 'too emphatic and for spoiling such passages as are too robust for their stage setting' (*The Times*). In earlier scenes the orchestra was more restrained than it had been before, and the opera was 'seen and heard as peaks of tension' (*The Times*).

Royal Opera House, Covent Garden
Grand Opera Season 1924
May 10, 1924, for four performances in German

	May 10, 16, 1924	*May 20, 1924*	*May 28, 1924*
Narraboth	Clemens	Gallos	Gallos
Prophet	Schipper	Schipper	Buers
Salome	Ljungberg	Ljungberg	Ljungberg
Herod	Kirchoff	Kirchoff	Kirchoff
Herodias	Olczewska	Olczewska	Olczewska
Conductor	Alwin	Alwin	Alwin

Scenery specially designed and painted by Ernest W. Millar (Staff Scenic Artist)
The Stage under the direction of Charles Moor

The casting of this season depended partly upon members of the Vienna State Opera (see *Rosenkavalier*, 1924); and since *Salome* had been a repertory piece on the Continent for many years, the production was well studied and mainly well sung.

Many of the London audience at the capacity first night were experiencing the opera for the first time, and since the original text had been reinstated, it became more coherent than before. Only the much ill-treated 'head' was again given special treatment: 'a dish covered with a disgustingly blood-stained napkin' (*The Times*) underneath which the object was supposed to be.

As Salome Mme. Göta Ljungberg was 'excellent in the part both as singer, dancer and actress' (*Illustrated London News*). 'She can be put beside Mme. Ackté, whose performance in years past created the chief sensation of the production. It is not necessary at this date to express wonder that Salome should execute the dance herself and not leave it to the première danseuse. Only an artist who has command of *Ton*, *Ticht und Tanz* can play the part adequately ... her sureness of voice and vividness of dramatic action told everything, and produced the impression of perverse sensuality which is the chief motive of the part' (*The Times*).

Hans Kirchoff, 'a magnificent Herod', and Göta Ljungberg, by working hard, were able 'to keep the attention concentrated on the main implications of the drama' (*The Times*).

It was a pity that Schipper's appearance did not match his voice. 'He was not ... a very impressive figure when he emerged' from the cistern, 'and he made little of the character beyond maintaining a statuesque dignity' (*The Times*).

Olczewska, making her London début as Herodias, and Clemens as Narraboth, were both very effective, as were the five wrangling Jews. The set was on familiar lines but was distinguished by a huge painted canvas awning over the acting area which gave the terrace a truly oriental effect.

For the first performance the opera was given alone, but for the remaining three, it was followed by Act III of *Siegfried*, sung by Florence Austral and Walter Kirchoff, and conducted by Alwin.

Royal Opera House, Covent Garden
Winter Opera Season, 1936/37
January 11, 1937, for three performances in German

	January 11, 15, 1937	January 20, 1937
Narraboth	Williams	Williams
Jokanaan	Schoeffler	Schoeffler
Salome	Ranczack	Schulz
Herod	Graarud	Graarud
Herodias	Kalter	Kalter
Conductor	Knappertsbusch	Knappertsbusch

Designer: Gabriel Volkoff
Producer: Hans Strobach (by permission of the State Opera Dresden)

A double bill of *Elektra* and *Salome* was intended to be the great attraction of this short season. After the success of the Dresden Company's visit (see *Rosenkavalier*, 1936; *Ariadne II*, 1936) Beecham asked Karl Böhm to conduct again, but he refused on the grounds that the idea of presenting both operas on the same evening offended his artistic principles. In the event, *Elektra* was not given because it was found impossible to cast, and *Salome* was conducted by Hans Knappertsbusch, who was only reluctantly granted a visa by the Nazis because of his lack of sympathy with them. The season was a failure since an influenza epidemic in London afflicted both audiences and singers, and resulted in several cast changes.

Mme. Ranczack, who sung Salome for the first and second performances, had 'a voice that tells least on the higher notes . . . had very little variety of colour, and a substantial presence which hardly suggests the shadow of a white rose in a silver mirror . . .' (*The Times*).

At the last performance, Else Schulz from Stuttgart was considered about equal in ability with Mme. Ranczack.

As Jokanaan (so called for the first time on the programme) 'Paul Schoeffler's fine voice told well . . . but those denunciations sung from the bottom of the cistern cannot have their full effect when so little of the words are heard. . . . The trap-door arrangement for entering the cistern, the very elementary dance of the Seven Veils, were details which emphasised the artificiality of the whole thing' (*The Times*). The sets were exact copies of the original Dresden production, borrowed from Germany for the occasion. Herr Hans Knappertsbusch conducted 'a well studied performance of the elaborate orchestration' (*The Times*). These are the only three performances of opera he has ever conducted in Britain.

Royal Opera House, Covent Garden
Visit of Vienna State Opera 1947
September 22, 1947, for three performances in German

	September 22, 26, 1947	September 30, 1947
Narraboth	Dermota	Friedrich
Jokanaan	Rothmüller	Rothmüller
Salome	L. Welitsch	Cebotari
Herod	Patzak	Patzak
Herodias	Hoengen	Hoengen
Conductor	Krauss	Krauss

Costumes by Hanni Bartsch   Producer: Josef Witte

The invigorating visit by the Vienna State Opera to Covent Garden consisted of five operas: three by Mozart, *Fidelio* and *Salome*. The most dynamic personality in the company was Ljuba Welitsch, and her portrayal of Strauss's 'sixteen-year-old Princess with the voice of Isolde'[1] was a superb performance. She 'could dominate stage and even orchestra. Her voice is hard for imperiousness, soft for seduction, and susceptible of every intermediate modulation. She has a commanding presence to act the part, and though she did not dance like a professional—Salome herself was presumably an amateur—she had the power of movement that held the eye while the ear was being borne along to the dramatic climax' (*The Times*).

Herr Clemens Krauss, 'perhaps the greatest of all Strauss conductors',[2] gave 'an equally sure and masterly realization of the complex score. . . . With these two crucial parts secure the opera succeeds in its aim of depicting the more recondite emotions from blood-lust to disgust' (*The Times*).

The opera was 'good to see. Sultry moonlight falls on corrupt and gilded splendours. We are thus offered some visual equivalent of the more imaginative pages in a flawed though still fascinating score' (*Observer*). 'The end was weak only in that Salome was not in this production buried beneath the weight of many shields but was merely struck down' (*The Times*).

Among the other parts Julius Patzak and Elisabeth Hoengen were finely cast and they sung admirably as Herod and Herodias. Hans Hotter was unable to sing Jokanaan as announced, and Marko Rothmüller (from Jay Pomeroy's Opera Company at the Cambridge Theatre) deputised for him at all performances. He was 'made up to look like a Byzantine Christ and sang with the authority of the prophet though his voice of just the right quality was only just big enough for the part' (*The Times*).

[1] *Recollections*, p. 151.
[2] Harold Rosenthal, *Two Centuries of Opera at Covent Garden*, London, 1958, p. 573.

At the third performance, that fine artist Maria Cebotari gave a beautifully studied though smaller-voiced interpretation of Salome. She later took part in the London Strauss Festival (see *Ariadne I*, 1947).

The presence and availability of Welitsch, and her immediate popularity in London, conspired towards the birth of the next production.

Royal Opera House, Covent Garden
1949/50 Season
November 11, 14, 18, 22, 26, 30, 1949, for six performances in English

Narraboth	Edgar Evans
Jokanaan	Schon
Salome	L. Welitsch
Herod	Lechleitner
Herodias	Shacklock
Conductor	Rankl

Scenery, costumes and special effects by Salvador Dali   Producer: Peter Brook

Looking back on the notorious Brook-Dali production of *Salome*, it is seen as a gamble that did not come off. At the time it stirred up one of those bitter and regrettable slanging matches in the Press, when the whole administration of the Opera House, and in particular Peter Brook, were strongly and mercilessly attacked, with Ernest Newman and Eric Blom leading the assault.

Sir David Webster has perceptively stated that a theatre or opera audience will accept almost any setting, but when the human figure is distorted because its costumes offend the sense and eye, first visual and then total disaster will follow. In this instance, so many offences were perpetrated in Salvador Dali's costumes and head-dresses, so many unnecessary tricks and effects failed to work anyhow, that a feeling of indignation was the basis of the controversy.

Peter Brook, who had achieved brilliant success as a theatre director in Birmingham, Stratford, London and Paris, took up the post of Director of Productions at Covent Garden against the advice of the man who 'brought him out'—Sir Barry Jackson. It was the *Salome* crisis that caused him to resign from Covent Garden. The reason why he employed Dali was, in his own words: 'because he is the only artist I know in the whole world whose natural style has both what one might call the erotic degeneracy of Strauss and the imagery of Wilde' (*Observer*). But Dali never came to London, never supervised his side of the production, never even saw it. Had he done so, many of the excesses might have been eliminated. The only significant aspect of the set, when considered after twelve years, is that it anticipated by two years something like the 'upturned saucer' of Bayreuth, which initiated a completely new form of Wagnerian stage production in 1951. Of course there can have been no connection—it just seems a strange coincidence of advanced thinking in stage design.

But like any *succès de scandale* this *Salome* was good box-office. The other incentive for hearing the opera was for seeing and hearing the Salome. Eric Blom said of her in the *Observer*: 'Ljuba Welitsch in the title part, except for the change of language, has remained much the same, even in appearance, as she was with the Vienna Company two years ago, taking her own line and hardly troubling to fit into the present production.[1] She sings magnificently. . . . One is impressed by her power of keeping so continually on the stretch.'

The Times was very complimentary to Mme. Welitsch and altogether quite polite about the production. The scheme of singing the opera in English (in an unspecified translation) fell down altogether because three of the principals were not English speakers. 'Kenneth Schon was not an adequate Jokanaan—his tone has not the body to represent a character of rock on which the heroine is to be wrecked' (*The Times*). The *Christian Science Monitor* observed that in the play Salome remarks of Jokanaan 'How wasted he is! He is like a thin ivory statue.' But since Schon was of operatic girth and weight, he 'must have been cast for the part by a surrealist. . . . Constance Shacklock, far too youthful to be the mother of a big girl like Salome, sang well out of a queer contraption of a costume'—'with a miniature Punch and Judy show for a head-dress. . . . The Herod of Franz Lechleitner, cruelly handi-capped by language and costume, is ineffectual' (*Observer*).

'The orchestra is second player to the protagonist. Dr. Rankl soon screwed his vastly expanded forces up to a tension that threatened to defeat its own end. The Viennese perform-ance kept it at a lower level of tone except for climaxes which helped the singers to be heard and the audiences to stay the course without cracking' (*The Times*).

This newspaper ended its notice: 'As a matter for the coroner it may be added that Salome came to her bad end not under a weight of shields but in the embrace of a kind of Nuremberg Maiden; whether this was Mr. Brook's or Mr. Dali's idea was not specified in the programme. But while some of the "special effects" attributed to Mr. Dali in the programme should be written off, he did revert to the original production by reintroducing the coloured execu-tioner,[2] whose mechanical, wooden arm came up from the cistern with the head balanced on it.'

Royal Opera House, Covent Garden
1950/51 Season
January 25, February 2, 1951, for two performances in English

Narraboth	Edgar Evans
Jokanaan	Rothmüller
Salome	Goltz
Herod	Carron
Herodias	Shacklock
Conductor	Rankl

Scenery painted by Clement Glock   Producer: Christopher West

[1] '"Dali does not know the opera", commented Welitsch; "it should be all light, not in darkness like the North Pole."' Rosenthal, *Two Centuries of Opera at Covent Garden*, p. 593.

[2] See p. 47.

54

Christel Goltz, leading soprano of the Berlin State Opera, made her first appearance in London as Salome. Comparison with Mme. Welitsch's performance was inevitable, but unfair since, as *The Times* said, 'Mme. Welitsch . . . made Salome a genius of depravity. Mme. Goltz begins in a lower key as an ordinary piece of nastiness who grows in viciousness with every bar of music.' Unfortunately the opera was again sung in English, which made things difficult for Mme. Goltz, and impossible for the audience as far as verbal comprehension went. But Mme. Goltz left nothing to the imagination when it came to gyrations, grimaces, a roll across the stage, and finally an extravagant exercise with the 'head' of Jokanaan. Vocally, though, Mme. Goltz achieved a success. So did Arthur Carron as Herod, and Marko Rothmüller as a truly Biblical figure of the Prophet. Praise was also given to Mr. Rankl and his orchestra, who had now taken the opera into their stride as a repertory piece.

As far as the settings were concerned they left much to be desired. After Mr. Dali's exotic and shadowy lavishness, the public saw a brightly-lit stage filled with pieces of scenery from the now discarded *Olympians* (Bliss-Priestly, 1949), and a Spanish archway (designed in 1934 for the second scene of Act II of *Fidelio* by Rex Whistler, but not used for many years).

Royal Opera House, Covent Garden
1950/51 Season
June 7, 12, 1951, for two performances in English

Narraboth	Edgar Evans
Jokanaan	Rothmüller
Salome	Varnay
Herod	Carron
Herodias	Coates
Conductor	Rankl

Scenery painted by Clement Glock   Producer: Christopher West

On two occasions since the war Ljuba Welitsch had set a standard for performing Salome. Christel Goltz had gone to the furthest visual extremes with the part, and now Astrid Varnay's performance seemed to be at the milk and water end of the scale. Although these three artists were well able to *sing* Strauss's music in an exemplary fashion, there is more to the role.

Ernest Newman, in a helpful notice in the *Sunday Times,* pointed out that Strauss 'did not want any of the stage parts, and especially that of Herod, to go beyond certain limits of frenzy. All that is needed in that respect, he said, is done by the orchestra.' Certainly Miss Varnay, with her usual intelligence, had taken this literally—perhaps too literally. But beyond a stereotyped range of clenched fists and repeated attitudes, Miss Varnay's interpretation was visually cold.

55

The only other change in the cast from the January performances was the Herodias. Sung by Edith Coates, for the first time in her career, she was able to add 'another termagant to her roles' (*The Times*).

Royal Opera House, Covent Garden
1951/52 Season
February 22, 1952, for one performance in English

Narraboth	Edgar Evans
Jokanaan	Rothmüller
Salome	Goltz
Herod	Carron
Herodias	Coates
Conductor	Tausky

Scenery painted by Clement Glock   Producer: Christopher West

This solitary performance of *Salome* was in preparation for its first tour of the provinces. It was not reviewed in London until its return in April.

Covent Garden Opera Company
Provincial Tour, 1952

This tour is important in the history of Welsh opera since it was the first during which a Strauss opera was presented in Wales. The première was *Rosenkavalier* (see p. 97), and two days later *Salome* was given.

Empire Theatre, Cardiff
February 28, 1952 (Welsh première), one performance in English and German

Narraboth	Edgar Evans
Jokanaan	Rothmüller
Salome	Dow
Herod	Carron
Herodias	Coates
Conductor	Tausky

The two principal South Wales newspapers praised the production and singing very highly. They both noted that Miss Dorothy Dow (an American soprano from Zürich) was called in as deputy and unfortunately sung in German. 'Vocally she was superb . . . and in the completely different technique of dancing . . . she was just as compelling' (*Western Mail*).

56

'Marko Rothmüller, as John the Baptist . . . appeared for only a short period and during that he dominated the scene using the greatest possible economy of action' (*South Wales Echo*).

Vilem Tausky was also complimented for his 'confident control of, and inspiration to, the large orchestra'.

Opera House, Manchester
March 12, 1952, in English

King's Theatre, Glasgow
March 19, 25, 1952, for two performances in English. Scottish première

Theatre Royal, Birmingham
April 8, 1952, in English

For all four performances:

Narraboth	Edgar Evans
Jokanaan	Rothmüller
Salome	Goltz
Herod	Carron
Herodias	Coates
Conductor	Tausky

Royal Opera House, Covent Garden
1951/52 Season
April 15, 1952, for two performances in English

	April 15, 1952	*April 24, 1952*
Narraboth	Edgar Evans	Edgar Evans
Jokanaan	Rothmüller	Rothmüller
Salome	Goltz	Dow
Herod	Carron	Carron
Herodias	Coates	Coates
Conductor	Tausky	Tausky

Scenery painted by Clement Glock   Producer: Christopher West

'Tausky's control of the performance was sure', said *The Times*, 'and the hateful yet fascinating drama progressed fluently. . . . Christel Goltz's interpretation of the title role is the mainstay of the performance; her singing has advanced in ease, reliability, range of colour, dramatic potency—in short, in artistry.' The same newspaper also found that Marko Rothmüller's Jokanaan 'is a tower of tonal and musical strength'.

The Press were not invited to Miss Dow's performance on April 24, and the event passed unnoticed by them.

Royal Opera House, Covent Garden
1953/54 Season
October 29, 1953, for three performances in English

	October 29, November 3, 1953	November 12, 1953
Narraboth	Edgar Evans	Edgar Evans
Jokanaan	Rothmüller	O. Kraus
Salome	L. Welitsch	L. Welitsch
Herod	Hannesson	Hannesson
Herodias	Coates	Coates
Conductor	Kempe	Kempe

Scenery painted by Clement Glock   Producer: Christopher West

'Mme. Welitsch bestrode the performance like a true Salome, six years after her first, stunning portrayal. There are gains and losses. . . . The voice now undergoes a certain strain.' *The Times* was being kind to Mme. Welitsch. At this, her last appearance in London, she was vocally an echo of her former strength, and unable to dominate the orchestra any more.

October 29 was the first performance under Rudolf Kempe as guest conductor to the resident company, the beginning of a long and valuable association.[1]

There was a rich portrayal of Herodias by Edith Coates and a dignified Jokanaan by Rothmüller. For the last performance Otakar Kraus was heard for the first time as the Prophet, a part he was now to make his own in London.

Royal Opera House, Covent Garden
1954/55 Season
July 5, 7, 9, 12, 1955, for four performances

Narraboth	Edgar Evans
Jokanaan	O. Kraus
Salome	Goltz
Herod	Seider
Herodias	Coates
Conductor	Kempe

Scenery painted by Clement Glock   Producer: Christopher West

This revival was unexceptional on the stage, but remarkable in the pit, thanks to Mr. Kempe's handling of the score and the orchestra.

Mme. Goltz was criticised for approaching the part 'in the spirit of a melodramatic vamp of the early flicks' who succeeded in producing 'not horror but the deep, deep yawn of

[1] See visit of Bavarian State Opera, p. 143.

provincial night-life' (*Observer*). Apart from the fact that Mme. Goltz could not remain still for one moment, there were absurdities of action and of translation, which Mr. Newman took up energetically in the *Sunday Times*.

King's Theatre, Edinburgh
Edinburgh Festival 1956. Visit of Hamburg State Opera
August 30, 1956, for five performances in German

	August 30, *September 1, 1956*	*September 4,* *1956*	*September 6,* *1956*	*September 8.* *1956*
Narraboth	Lehnert	Lehnert	Lehnert	Lehnert
Jokanaan	Bröcheler	Metternich	Bröcheler	Metternich
Salome	Pilarczyk	Pilarczyk	Borkh	Borkh
Herod	Markwort	Markwort	Markwort	Markwort
Herodias	Eriksdotter	Eriksdotter	Eriskdotter	Eriksdotter
Conductor	Ludwig	Ludwig	Ludwig	Ludwig

Designer: Alfred Siercke   Producer: Wolf Völker

The planned casting of this opera went adrift and instead of Goltz singing the first two Salomes and Pilarczyk the rest, Goltz did not sing at all, and Borkh came to perform the last two. Helmut Melchert, who was to have sung four Herods, sung none. The main interest was to hear Pilarczyk's interpretation in a well rehearsed production which was familiar to the singers.

The set, by Alfred Siercke, was highly successful and 'showed a sultry night on the palace forecourt' (*The Times*), while the production was finely thought out and realised by Wolf Völker with unity of conception carried out in every detail of performance.

Unfortunately Pilarczyk's voice proved to be inadequate to the task, in that she was 'unable for much of the evening to project her voice properly and she had great difficulty in cutting through the enormous mass of sound that came from Leopold Ludwig's orchestra' (*Opera*). That a smaller voice can be effective in this part was remembered from Maria Cebotari's performance in September 1947.

Visually, though, Pilarczyk 'looks and acts more like a young Salome than anyone for years' (*Opera*) 'making the disgust of the disgusting Herod and the envious admiration of the viperish Herodias an inevitable reaction to such a personality' (*The Times*).

There were no weak spots in the casting, and in particular Eriksdotter and Markwort as Herodias and Herod were a dissolute pair.

At the first performance Caspar Bröcheler's voice sounded well from the cistern and he had an impressive appearance to match it. At later performances Josef Metternich sang Jokanaan's music with a beautiful tone, but did not look sufficiently imposing.

A good production touch made Herodias try to stop Herod from having Salome crushed to death. Musically Ludwig 'controlled his forces from a low plane of tone, though the complex counterpoint came through and the tension mounted gradually . . . into a texture that felt as if it would have smothered us . . .' had not the curtain come down when it did (*The Times*).

Royal Opera House, Covent Garden
1958/59 Season
January 28, 31, February 2, 4, 10, 1959, for five performances in English

Narraboth	Edgar Evans
Jokanaan	O. Kraus
Salome	Pilarczyk
Herod	Witte
Herodias	Shacklock
Conductor	Goodall

Scenery painted by Clement Glock   Production supervised by Ande Anderson

Two and a half years later, Helga Pilarczyk seemed to have increased the power of her voice at the expense of its quality, for the *Sunday Times* said: 'The one thing that for the musician can redeem the work is a stream of clear soprano tone . . . and she sings the music with much art; but her tone is seldom quite pure.' Andrew Porter in the *Financial Times* said she 'is capable: but that is not enough. Her voice last night had little beauty in it, no bloom, no radiance, and often it lost quality altogether'.

There was some fine singing from Otakar Kraus as Jokanaan although he 'hardly seemed a romantic enough Prophet to inflame Salome's desires' (*Financial Times*). But he had 'all the fervour and fanaticism the part demands' (*Sunday Times*). Erich Witte's Herod, sung in lucid English, did not quite come up to expectations; but Constance Shacklock 'sung and sustained Herodias's music and showed a firm grasp of the character'. Reginald Goodall conducted ably.

The production was 'a bizarre hodge-podge of Dali and other things' and dramatically 'not only anonymous but haphazard' in the court scene (*The Times*).

Royal Opera House, Covent Garden
1959/60 Season
November 13, 1959 (fiftieth performance at Covent Garden) for three performances in German

	November 13, 16, 1959	*November 18, 1959*
Narraboth	Edgar Evans	Edgar Evans
Jokanaan	O. Kraus	O. Kraus
Salome	Borkh	Borkh
Herod	Melchert	Eschert
Herodias	Hoengen	Hoengen
Conductor	Kempe	Kempe

Scenery painted by Clement Glock   Production supervised by Ande Anderson

In *Opera*,[1] John Warrack went to some pains to point out that it is the cruel streak running through romantic characters in nineteenth-century literature which is the root of Wilde's and Strauss's *Salome*. The terror lies in the fact that 'she is a sixteen-year-old virgin; it is a sulky child who obstinately insists on having the man's head off his shoulders if she can't get it while it's on them.' Mr. Warrack's object in this was to show how basically wrong Miss Borkh's interpretation had been, with its 'depraved Elektra-like figure, lunging about the stage with eyes rolling horribly and lips drooling in anticipation of satisfying a familiar blood-lust'. *The Times* stated: 'It is an unstable interpretation, erotically exaggerated sometimes to caricature (her attire disadvantageously made her look like Mr. Tony Curtis in *Some Like It Hot*), and losing much in vividness by her surely too modest decision to send a deputy (Ann Parson) for the dance sequence.' Musically, however, Miss Borkh was secure, accurate and possessed a proud vocal ring.

The two characters of Herod and Herodias (Melchert and Hoengen) were described by *The Times*: Herod as 'a virtuoso piece of vocal acting, feather-brained rather than depraved, completely extravert and curiously, ludicrously real' and Herodias 'a flapper whose brainless gaiety had sinister implications conveyed with equal virtuosity of voice and deportment'. 'Otakar Kraus, as versatile and musicianly as always, made a noble Jokanaan' (*Opera*), while Edgar Evans was again most effective as Narraboth. Kempe produced voluptuous playing from the orchestra but these assets could not save the total effect.

At the last performance Hasso Eschert deputised at short notice for Helmut Melchert, as he had done for Jon Vickers at the 1957 Television performance.[2]

Summary of Performances

London	57
Cardiff	1
Manchester	1
Glasgow	2
Edinburgh	1
TOTAL	62

[1] Vol. XI, No. 1, pp. 61-2.
[2] See p. 176.

DER ROSENKAVALIER

DER ROSENKAVALIER

THIS WAS THE FIRST OPERA in Strauss's genial style; the second in the fruitful collaboration with von Hofmannsthal; the fifth in the canon of Strauss operas; and by far the most successful, financially for its creators, and in popular demand.

The first mention of *Der Rosenkavalier* in the correspondence between Strauss and von Hofmannsthal occurs in a letter from Hofmannsthal dated February 11, 1909, when he says:

'Now something which is (as I hope) of far greater importance to the two of us. I have spent three quiet afternoons here drafting the full and entirely original scenario for an opera, full of burlesque situations and characters, with lively action, pellucid almost like a pantomime. There are opportunities in it for lyrical passages, for fun and humour, even for a small ballet. I find the scenario enchanting and Count Kessler,[1] with whom I discussed it, is delighted with it. It contains two big parts, one for baritone and another for a graceful girl dressed up as a man, *à la* Farrar or Mary Garden. Period: the old Vienna under the Empress Maria Theresa.

'After Sunday I shall be in Berlin, Schadowstrasse 4.

'Shall we meet? (But not at a party, that is pointless.)'[2]

From then on and until January 12, 1911 (two weeks before the première of the opera) over sixty letters passed between them on the subject of *Rosenkavalier*, originally to be called *Ochs von Lerchenau*.

Strauss required many alterations to be made to the libretto as it came to him, act by act, and while von Hofmannsthal found this tiresome, he was more than anxious to satisfy the composer. The manner of solving their various problems, as we read in the *Correspondence*, tested and proved their ability to work together.

Von Hofmannsthal wrote to Strauss upon two occasions towards the middle and end of 1910: 'I pray you are content—for myself I must say I so enjoyed working on this piece that it almost saddens me to have to write "Curtain".'[3] And later, 'your music gives me immense pleasure. It is like a festoon of many pretty flowers and so marvellously organic in the transitions.'[4]

When it was decided—and ultimately arranged—to present the opera for the first time in

[1] German diplomat and co-author with Hofmannsthal of *The Legend of Joseph*, the Ballet for Diaghilev. Von Hofmannsthal often sought and greatly respected Kessler's opinions.

[2] *Correspondence*, p. 27.

[3] *Correspondence*, p. 58.

[4] *Ibid.*, p. 74.

6

Dresden, Count Seebach, the Intendant there, found himself shocked at three particular passages in the text, to be spoken by Ochs.[1] He also wanted the Marschallin to be *out* of bed at the rise of the curtain on the first act. Strauss was annoyed at what he considered false modesty and hypocrisy, and the compromise was that of the three offending Ochs passages all would be omitted in the libretto but two retained in the score.

In September, von Hofmannsthal, in suggesting a sub-title for the work says: 'The title *Rosenkavalier* seems to strike people as very pretty and attractive, as I hear from all sides. If you agree, I shall call my book edition *Burlesque for Music*, and the definitive title of the whole work is

DER ROSENKAVALIER
Burlesque Opera in 3 Acts
by Hugo von Hofmannsthal
Music by Richard Strauss

P.S. "Burlesque opera" gives us back something of what the title "Ochs von Lerchenau" was to have conveyed.'[2]

To this Strauss replied on (probably) September 12 in a postscript: 'Subtitle: "Comedy for Music" is by far the best and freest. "Burlesque Opera" is impossible; after all, there's nothing burlesque about it. Just think what the public would expect: Offenbach, *Mikado*, etc. "Opera" by itself would also do. But let's keep "Comedy for Music": it's clear and new and free!'[3]

Ultimately the title became

DER ROSENKAVALIER
Comedy for music in three Acts by Hugo von Hofmannsthal
Music by Richard Strauss
Opus 59

There were difficulties, too, over casting. Ochs caused trouble in person as he had done in the title. Perron, who was already rehearsing, was proving little more than adequate, and in Strauss's words '. . . the opera must not be allowed out with a merely *adequate* Ochs. Whether Mayr will be ready to take it depends largely on Schalk; to snatch him away from Weingarten[4] would be a *cura posteria*. That leaves Bender (Munich), who is available. . . . In case you and Reinhardt do not succeed in grooming Perron for the part, I give you full powers of veto to cancel the première with Perron on the 26th.[5] The latter is such a first-class artist that he will understand and share our misgivings. Do treat him tactfully—he's trying terribly hard—but at the same time be implacable, for the fate of our opera is at stake.'[6]

[1] Von Hofmansthal called them 'rather downright words'. *Correspondence*, p. 59.

[2] *Ibid.*, p. 67.

[3] *Correspondence*, p. 68.

[4] Schalk and Weingarten were principal conductors at the Vienna Opera, Richard Mayr a principal bass-baritone there.

[5] Jan. 26, 1911, the première of *Rosenkavalier* in Dresden.

[6] *Correspondence*, p. 71.

Von Hofmannsthal heard from Schalk in Vienna that Mayr would not be available until two weeks after the opening date, but that then Schalk said he would leave *'nothing* to be desired'. Von Hofmannsthal deplored the casting as Ochs of the 'almost spectral' Perron, and went to look at Bender in Munich, of whom he says in a letter of January 8, 1911 (only eighteen days before the advertised première), 'I have just learnt to my sorrow that Bender is also no Falstaff, is in fact anything but, and therefore no Ochs—at least in no way naturally fitted for the part. Oh well, if all bass buffos are long and lean and only the Quinquins[1] thick and fat, I may as well close down!'[2]

Perron was the first Ochs, and Bender 'not an ideal Ochs, but still a very good one, all the same',[3] became a kind of special understudy, and took over later. (He played Ochs in London in 1924, see p. 75.)

But the greatest difficulties of all—libretto and score apart—lay on the stage. Georg Toller, the staff producer at Dresden, was found very early on in rehearsals to be quite inadequate. Once more the success of the opera was held by Strauss and von Hofmannsthal to matter more than anything else, and with reluctant permission from Count Seebach, Max Reinhardt was brought in from Berlin as adviser. The condition was that Reinhardt must not set foot on the stage. As Strauss himself recalled later[4]: 'Reinhardt came without making demands, and, Jew and art enthusiast that he was, even accepted the above condition, and thus we all met on the rehearsal stage, Reinhardt as a modest spectator, whilst I in my clumsy way showed the singers as best I could how to play their parts. After a while Reinhardt could be observed whispering to Frau von der Osten[5] in a corner of the hall and then again with Miss Siems,[6] Perron,[7] etc.

'The next day they came to the rehearsal transformed into fully-fledged actors. Thereupon Seebach graciously permitted Reinhardt to direct operations on the stage instead of watching the rehearsal from the stalls. The result was a new style of opera and a perfect performance in which the trio in particular (Siems, von der Osten, Nast[8]) delighted everybody.'

The English Première 1913

Thomas Beecham's plan to take a lease of Drury Lane and present the Diaghilev Ballet there in 1911 was not carried out because the threat was sufficient to force the Grand Opera Syndicate at Covent Garden into inviting him onto their Board. Thus freed from administrative duties, Beecham was now able to devote more time to conducting. In 1912 the advent

[1] *Quinquin* is the Marschallin's pet name for Octavian in the opera.
[2] *Correspondence*, p. 73.
[3] *Ibid.*, p. 74.
[4] *Recollections*, p. 157.
[5] Octavian.
[6] Marschallin.
[7] Baron Ochs.
[8] Sophie.

of Oscar Hammerstein to London to present opera in a new house which he built himself,[1] caused Beecham 'to leave the newcomer in unopposed control of the ground, quit the stage for a while, and return to the calmer life of the concert room'.[2]

While in Berlin in 1912, introducing Elgar and Delius to the Germans, Beecham met Strauss and promised that he would present *Der Rosenkavalier* in London during the early part of 1913.

Beecham records[3] that the Lord Chamberlain's Office once more became interested in the news that another Strauss opera was on the way: '. . . they had discovered the presence of a bed in a remote part of the stage in the third act and were worried about some equivocal reference to it in the text. . . . I was given the option of two courses. Either the bed could be exhibited without any reference being made to it, or it could be hidden away from sight and we could sing about it as much as we liked. As it was easier to move the furniture around than to tamper with the score of the work, I accepted the second alternative, and I have always regarded this as a nearly perfect example of our British love of compromise.'

At the beginning of January Beecham issued his prospectus with dates and casts all complete. The first performance of *Der Rosenkavalier* beat the box-office record of *Salome* by selling out in an hour, and the remaining seven performances were as good as sold out after the excitement of the première on January 29.

The Story of the Opera

The opera opens in the boudoir of a certain Princess who, during her husband's absence, is amusing herself with a youthful cavalier, Octavian by name. An urgent love scene is interrupted by the sound of voices outside, and the Princess, thinking her husband has returned unexpectedly, persuades Octavian to disguise himself in the clothes of her maid. The owner of the voice, however, happens to be the impecunious Baron Ochs, who is anxious to consult the Princess in regard to a proposed match with Sophie, the daughter of a vulgar millionaire. There is a realistic little toilet scene, at which the supposed maid assists, and is ogled by the Baron. Octavian becomes the Baron's rose cavalier—that is to say, he is entrusted with the delivery to Sophie of the rose which the Baron duly dispatches as a *gage d'amour*. Of course, the inevitable happens and Octavian and Sophie fall madly in love with each other. Tender passages between the pair are interrupted by the arrival of the Baron, and there is a tremendous rumpus as the result of Octavian having slightly wounded his rival. A ruse finally sets matters straight. Octavian is persuaded to assume once more girl's clothes and to make an assignation with the Baron. At a critical moment the door is burst open, and the old roué—discovered under compromising circumstances—is sent about his business.

(*Argument from Programme of January 29, 1913, Royal Opera House, Covent Garden.*)

[1] The London Opera House, later the Stoll Theatre, Kingsway. It was demolished in 1958 and a small theatre within an office block on the same site was opened on June 23, 1960. Subsequently, only films were shown there.

[2] *Beecham*, p. 109.

[3] *Ibid.*, p. 114.

68

Royal Opera House, Covent Garden

January 29, 1913 (British première) for eight performances in German

	January 29, February 1, 1913	February 5, 1913	February 8, 1913
Octavian	von der Osten	Bosetti	Bosetti
Marschallin	Siems	Petzl-Perard	Petzl-Perard
Baron Ochs	Knüpfer	Gmür	Knüpfer
Valzacchi	Bechstein	Bechstein	Bechstein
Annina	Gura-Hummel	Gura-Hummel	Gura-Hummel
Tenor Singer	Blamey	Blamey	Blamey
von Faninal	Brodersen	Brodersen	Brodersen
Sophie	Dux	Dux	Dux
Conductor	Beecham	Beecham	Beecham

	February 12, 1913	February 20, 27 (*mat.*), 1913	March 8, 1913
Octavian	Bosetti	Sanden	Gutheil-Schoder
Marschallin	Petzl-Perard	Iracema-Brugelmann	Wolf
Baron Ochs	Pacyna	Knüpfer	Knüpfer
Valzacchi	Bechstein	Bechstein	Bechstein
Annina	Gura-Hummel	Gura-Hummel	Gura-Hummel
Tenor Singer	Blamey	Blamey	Blamey
von Faninal	Hermann Gura	Wiedermann	Hermann Gura
Sophie	Dux	Dux	Dux
Conductor	Schilling-Ziemssen	Schilling-Ziemssen	Beecham

Costumes supplied by Fisher Ltd. The opera produced by Hermann Gura
Furniture by Waring's

Whatever epithets had been applied to the three other Strauss operas already performed in London, the critics were unanimous in their praise of the new work:

'*The Rose Bearer* is not only brilliant, it is beautiful; not only beautiful but finely considered —the ripe expression of genius' (*Illustrated London News*).

'It is the most prodigal and elaborate sacrifice ever offered the Muse of Frivolity' (*Daily Telegraph*).

'. . . *der Rosenkavalier*, surely the wittiest opera that ever emanated from the brain of a musician' (*Morning Post*), and 'The Musical Sensation of the Hour—this quaint eighteenth-century Viennese story in music provides an entertainment upon which Mr. Beecham is to be warmly congratulated' (*Tatler*).

One or two of the critics—who had been to performances abroad—were aware of a few small imperfections, due partly to short rehearsal-time. Since there were six different casts of principals in the eight performances, they might seem to have justified six different notices, but unfortunately only the first performance has gone down in journalistic history to mark the initial season of the *Rosenkavalier*.

The *Daily Telegraph* noticed that there were cuts in the Baron's monologues in Act I—something which was to be discussed with ferocity later on, in 1931—and that the scenery was not quite up to the standard of that seen in Germany. And while the Act II set seemed satisfactory, 'the room in the inn was surely a little too beautiful for its purpose' (*The Times*).

Even though the language barrier prevented a complete understanding by the majority of the audience of what was being said on the stage, this was far less of a problem than in many other operas, and 'in all conscience, the witticism in Strauss's opera is clear enough, on the whole, for the enjoyment of any race that has a soul for wit' (*The Times*).

Yet it was observed that the comedy is probably too drawn out, and it is this which may fail 'to allow *Rosenkavalier* the overwhelming success it has attained to in other European countries'.

No one, after all, took exception to the beds in Act I and Act III, nor to some of Baron Ochs's remarks and activities. It was noted that von Hofmannsthal's discretion had allowed these situations to be carried off with the utmost tact and elimination of offence.

The three principals at the first performance were highly praised. The *Daily Telegraph* found that 'Mme. von der Osten's splendid, gallant voice did much to reconcile one to the objectionable if inevitable travesty of a woman acting a man's part'; and the *Daily News* (Kalisch) found that 'the presence in the cast of Frl. Siems, who had created the part of the Princess at Dresden, and of Frl. von der Osten, the original Octavian, lent strength, for both are splendid artists, and both were at their best. It is impossible to imagine the pathos of one and the crânerie of the other better rendered. Then Herr Knüpfer is an ideal Ochs, with his mixture of aristocratic haughtiness and clumsy licentiousness. . . . Frl. Dux, of Berlin, was delightful as Sophie, the ingénue.' The smaller parts were said to be well played, and no doubt improved greatly through these eight performances, as the same singers remained.

The three musical high-spots of the opera were singled out for comment: the Marschallin's monologue in Act I, 'the tender wistfulness of it, the smile that is so near to weeping are irresistible—it is a wonderful, original scene'; the Presentation of the Silver Rose[1] in Act II 'as fine a musical description of what might be called patrician splendour as has ever been put on paper'; and the end of the third act 'the crown of the whole' (*Daily News*).

Beecham was highly praised for making possible the production of the work, and in

[1] The idea of the Silver Rose as an emblem of proposal of matrimony has been variously described as an invention of von Hofmannsthal's, and as a real Viennese custom. It is neither of these.

In 1049, during the reign of Leo IX, this Pope instituted the giving of a *golden* rose to virtuous and noble ladies. It was stopped by Pius X in 1903, and not reintroduced until Pope Pius XI conferred it upon the Queen of Spain in 1925.

No doubt von Hofmannsthal knew of this, and brought the poetic quality of it into his libretto by introducing a rose into the armorial bearings of Lerchenau, thereby making the *silver* rose a charming and original gift of the impecunious Baron Ochs.

particular for his conducting from memory 'if the expression is at all apt in the circumstances'. 'His influence was all pervading' (*Daily Telegraph*).

The Opera House was full to capacity for the première, and seats were at prices which could not possibly assure a financial success. But at Beecham's insistence, lower prices made the work available to many less affluent members of the public. As to the artistic success of *Der Rosenkavalier*, there was no doubt whatsoever.

The Rose Bearer on Provincial Tour 1913
The Denhof Grand Opera Company
Projected visits to six English and three Scottish Cities[1]

Prince of Wales Theatre, Birmingham
September 20, 24, 26, 1913

Octavian	Schiller
Marschallin	Nicholls
Baron Ochs	Pacyna
Valzacchi	Bechstein
Annina	Terry
Tenor Singer	Blamey
von Faninal	Austin
Sophie	Hatchard
Conductor	Schilling-Ziemssen

Designer and Producer not stated

On September 20, 1913, *Rosenkavalier* (as *The Rose Bearer*) was performed in English for the first time, and it was also the first provincial presentation of the opera. The translation by Alfred Kalisch (music critic of the *Daily News*) was 'a model of lucidity and singableness', according to the *Birmingham Mail*, and no difficulties were considered, at that time, to have arisen in the course of translation.

The most interesting singer was thought to be Arthur Pacyna, who had 'a bass voice of more than usual beauty and power, and a stage technique quite assured, and a sense of comedy —broad or low or subtle—which are priceless. . . . He is one of Mr. Denhof's "finds" and opera-in-English is all the richer.' Those who attended the first performance of the opera in Birmingham found it to be 'a great experience'.

Theatre Royal, Manchester

	September 29, 1913	October 4 (*mat.*), 1913
Octavian	Schiller	Schiller
Marschallin	Nicholls	Nicholls

[1] For details of the management of the Denhof Tour, see pp. 24 and 26.

	September 29, 1913	October 4 (mat.), 1913
Baron Ochs	Pacyna	Pacyna
Valzacchi	Bechstein	Bechstein
Annina	Terry	Terry
Tenor Singer	Blamey	de Sousa
von Faninal	Ranalow	Austin
Sophie	Hatchard	Hatchard
Conductor	Schilling-Ziemssen	Schilling-Ziemssen

(For subsequent events at the end of the first week at Manchester, see pp. 27 to 28.)

Lyceum Theatre, Sheffield
October 15, 1913

Octavian	Schiller
Marschallin	Nicholls
Baron Ochs	Pacyna
Valzacchi	Bechstein
Annina	Terry
Tenor Singer	Blamey
von Faninal	Ranalow
Sophie	Hatchard
Conductor	Schilling-Ziemssen

Grand Theatre, Leeds
October 25, 1913

Octavian	Schiller
Marschallin	Nicholls
Baron Ochs	Pacyna
Valzacchi	Bechstein
Annina	Terry
Tenor Singer	Blamey
von Faninal	Austin
Sophie	Hatchard
Conductor	Schilling-Ziemssen

Shakespeare Theatre, Liverpool
The Denhof Operatic Festival
October 27, November 1 (mat.), 1913
  Cast as in Sheffield

Theatre Royal, Manchester
November 6, 1913
Cast as in Leeds

Theatre Royal, Newcastle upon Tyne
November 14, 1913
Cast as in Leeds

King's Theatre, Edinburgh
The Denhof Opera Festival
November 17 (Scottish première), November 22 (mat.), 1913
Cast as in Sheffield

'*The Rose Bearer* was given pride of place in the list of operas which it is proposed to present in the coming fortnight. Mr. Thomas Beecham, who is understood to have taken over the financial responsibilities of Mr. Denhof's operatic enterprise, was not in the conductor's box last evening but his place was ably filled by Mr. Schilling-Ziemssen . . .' (*Scotsman*). The Denhof tour finished, prematurely, in Edinburgh, having visited six English and one Scottish Cities.

In 1913 Beecham had engaged Diaghilev's company of singers and dancers to appear in London, and had unsuccessfully attempted to influence the Grand Opera Syndicate (of which he was a director) to present Chaliapin in Russian opera during the summer season. Beecham therefore resigned, booked Drury Lane, and with the financial support of his father, Sir Joseph, had a most successful season there.[1]

In 1914 Beecham again booked 'the Lane' for the summer, and prefaced his second Russian opera season with six performances of *Der Rosenkavalier*, and three of *Die Zauberflöte*.

Theatre Royal, Drury Lane
May 20, 1914, for six performances in German

	May 20, 23, 26, 28, 1914	June 2, 1914	June 4, 1914
Octavian	Uhr	Lippe	Lippe
Marschallin	Siems	Siems	Hempel
Baron Ochs	Knüpfer	Bohnen	Bohnen
Valzacchi	Bechstein	Bechstein	Bechstein

[1] Diaghilev's reactions to Beecham's methods are described thus: '. . . Beecham . . . made an arrangement with me which I confess worried me somewhat, for it was merely a letter authorising me . . . to engage the best artists —the whole of Russia—while he himself footed the bill. When on one occasion he wanted Chaliapin, Smirnov, Kuznetzova, Nijinsky and Karsavina all to appear in the same programme, and I modestly protested, saying that the expense of such a production would be unheard of, he merely said it was none of my business.' Serge Lifar, *Serge Diaghilev*, 1940, pp. 254-5.

73

	May 20, 23, 26, 28 1914	June 2, 1914	June 4 1914
Annina	Terry	Terry	Terry
Tenor Singer	Marescotti	Marescotti	Marescotti
von Faninal	Brodersen	Brodersen	Brodersen
Sophie	Dux	Lehmann	Lehmann
Conductor	Beecham	Beecham	Beecham

Costumes by Fishers; Furniture by Waring's; Special Act Drop designed and painted by Vladimir Polunin   Producer and Stage Manager: Charles Moor

While these performances did not rival those of 1913, they were played to a receptive and perceptive audience, more familiar with the work.

The Times, in discussing Frl. Siems, 'missed the quality of tone which she has had and found a thinness, even a harshness, which was unpleasant'. However, she triumphed in her Act I monologue. Knüpfer was again complimented upon his skill with the part of Ochs, and Brodersen, too, was thought to be making the best of the 'boring part' of von Faninal.

The newcomer, Fr. Charlotte Uhr, 'is a great acquisition. At once her beautiful voice held the interest of the audience and her singing, always pure and true, had dramatic character. . . . To hear her voice with that of Fr. Claire Dux in the duet in Act II was a great treat.' Beecham says of Uhr's Octavian 'the best I have ever known'.[1] Claire Dux, as Sophie, made an even greater impact than in 1913. Her 'voice was remarkable for two qualities, a perfect legato, and a phenomenal breath control . . .' said Beecham.[2]

The *Morning Post* said of the 'wonderful performance' that from Thomas Beecham who conducted (from memory) '. . . . down to the delightful monkey which appeared in the Marschallin's boudoir, the spirit that pervaded the performance was in glorious and perfect sympathy with the work'.

The Times recorded that 'The amazing Beecham opera season . . . opened last night with a crowded house and the brilliant, captivating, hilariously unedifying and cynical *Rose Cavalier* of Richard Strauss conducted by Thomas Beecham. . . . Strauss is a giant among our music makers and one bows to so large a nature even when squirming at some foibles such as the different outbursts of horseplay. . . .' Charlotte Uhr was complimented on her 'fetching assumption of manliness: decidedly one of the best of Octavians'.

At the last two performances Claire Dux was replaced by an unknown soprano called Lotte Lehmann, who, as Sophie, failed to impress her audience and disappeared back to Austria.

Ten years later, almost to the day, in a new age, robbed of much of its dignity by the First World War, *Rosenkavalier* again appeared in London.

[1] *Beecham*, p. 127.
[2] *Ibid.*, p. 126.

Royal Opera House, Covent Garden
May 21, 1924, for six performances in German (two more than announced)

	May 21, 23, 26, 1924	May 29, 1924	June 2, 3, 1924
Octavian	Reinhardt	Reinhardt	Reinhardt
Marschallin	Lehmann	Leider	Lehmann
Baron Ochs	Mayr	Bender	Jerger
Valzacchi	Gallos	Gallos	Gallos
Annina	Jung	Jung	Jung
Tenor Singer	Fischer-Niemann	Fischer-Niemann	Fischer-Niemann
von Faninal	Habich	Habich	Renner
Sophie	Schumann	Schumann	Schumann
Conductor	Walter	Walter	Walter

Scenery specially designed and painted for this production by Ernest Woodroffe Millar
The stage under the direction of Charles Moor

The first of a succession of over thirty performances established the work in even more popular favour and with a cast that gave us an outstanding pair of characters who set their seal on future interpretations until the second World War broke out. They were Mayr and Lehmann.

The Grand Opera Syndicate at Covent Garden engaged Lotte Lehmann to sing the Marschallin. She did not tell them that she had never sung the role before.

The fact that Lehmann, as well as Elisabeth Schumann (Sophie), Delia Reinhardt (Octavian) and Richard Mayr (Baron Ochs), all came from Vienna was not entirely a coincidence. Opera politics had first decided upon a visit from the Vienna State Opera in 1924; national politics had cancelled this visit, but several of the artists were able to come to London. How fortunate for the course of this opera in England that they did.

The first London performance of *Rosenkavalier* in 1913, and the performance of May 21, 1924, are still said by those who at first hand remember them, to be the best ever performed in Britain. *The Times* even went further on this occasion and said it was the best performance 'of *any*[1] opera seen and heard at Covent Garden in living memory. . . .The cast was admirably chosen and the whole thing was exquisitely dovetailed together.'

The outstanding principal was reckoned by *The Times* to be Richard Mayr, 'whose Baron Ochs is famous, but who was seen and heard in this country now for the first time. His voluble speeches to the Princess and his amorous asides to her supposed maid, his coarse courting of his bride, his fuss over his wound, and his Falstaffian delight in the faked assignation were all of a piece. . . . It is easy to have too much of Baron Ochs but we never had too much of Herr Mayr for his buffoonery never obliterated the music.

'The three principal ladies,' *The Times* went on, 'all sang with purity and complete

[1] Author's italics.

understanding of their parts. The only fault was in the fact that their voices were not sufficiently contrasted in *timbre*. One felt that Mme. Reinhardt's voice coalesced too easily with each of the ladies who arouse in turn the passion of the susceptible Octavian.'

Richard Mayr has been described as having a 'rather woolly' voice. A superb character actor, and one of the best comedians in the world, his Ochs von Lerchenau was his masterpiece, a part which won him world fame.[1]

The success of Lotte Lehmann as the Marschallin was a vindication of her previous appearance in 1914, and the first of a serious of marvellous and ever blooming interpretations. No one, before or since, has matched her performance at the end of Act I, nor in the utterly noble way in which she dismissed Ochs in Act III.

If Delia Reinhardt 'did not cut quite the boyish figure', and seemed more naturally to be dressed as a girl than a boy, that was a minor consideration considering the excellence of her performance as a whole.

The opera was the outstanding success of the 1924 season.

Because of the extra two performances, some changes in cast were unavoidable. On May 29, Frida Leider (so far known to London audiences only as Brünnhilde and Isolde), was 'dignified and wistful', and Paul Bender was the new Ochs.

For the last two performances Alfred Jerger was vocally a good Ochs, but audiences who had already seen and heard Mayr were educated up to the highest standards.

The 1924 season turned out to be financially disastrous to the Syndicate, and it was only by the intervention of Mr. and Mrs. Samuel Courtauld as backers that the 1925 season was made possible. Until 1933, the reformed Syndicate, under the able management of Lt. Col. Eustace Blois, took on a new lease of life.

Despite the late start caused by these revisions to the management structure, familiar conductors and singers were re-engaged, and the famous cast for *Rosenkavalier*, under Bruno Walter's baton, opened the season on May 18.

Royal Opera House, Covent Garden
May 18, 1925, for five performances in German

	May 18, 22, 28, June 12, 1925	June 10, 1925
Octavian	Reinhardt	Reinhardt
Marschallin	Lehmann	Kappel
Baron Ochs	Mayr	Mayr
Valzacchi	Reiss	Reiss
Annina	Paalen	Olczewska
Tenor Singer	Mummery	Mummery
von Faninal	Habich	Habich

[1] Mayr was in private life a brewer, and a fairly rich man. His hobby was walking between Austrian inns, tasting their beer as an expert.

	May 18, 22, 28, June 12, 1925	June 10, 1925
Sophie	Schumann	Schumann
Conductor	Walter	Walter

Scenery specially designed and painted for this production by Ernest Woodroffe Millar
The Stage under the direction of Charles Moor

'The cast was largely that of last year, with Herr Mayr and the three principal ladies who appeared then. All are first-rate singers whose representations are so assured that we have only to express pleasure in hearing them again. Mme. Lotte Lehmann moves us most in that passage where the Princess first realises that youth is not to be held. Mme. Delia Reinhardt plays the impulsive Octavian with charm and vigour, and the love duet sung by her with Mme. Elisabeth Schumann in the second act was so satisfying that the incursion of the spies which stopped it seemed more than usually annoying.

'It is Strauss's fault that we get too much of the soprano voice in Der Rosenkavalier and the excess is emphasised by a similarity of timbre in these three voices. . . . English singers, it is worthwhile to note, are not excluded from Covent Garden. They did excellent work in minor parts and in the chorus' (The Times).

Bruno Walter was singled out for especial praise in his handling of the opera and his deep understanding of the idiom.[1]

At the fifth performance on June 10, Gertrud Kappel replaced Lehmann as the Marschallin but was not remarkable; in the comprimaria role of Annina, however, Maria Olczewska was outstandingly good.

Royal Opera House, Covent Garden
May 2, 1927, for five performances in German

	May 2, 10, 12, 27, 1927	May 18, 1927
Octavian	Reinhardt	Reinhardt
Marschallin	Lehmann	Lehmann
Baron Ochs	Mayr	Mayr
Valzacchi	Reiss	Reiss
Annina	von Hoesslin	von Hoesslin
Tenor Singer	Mummery	Mummery
von Faninal	Habich	Habich
Sophie	Schumann	Schumann
Conductor	Walter	Heger

Scenery specially designed and painted for this production by Ernest Woodroffe Millar
The Stage under the direction of Charles Moor

[1] At rehearsals of Der Rosenkavalier at Covent Garden, the orchestra always greeted Bruno Walter on his way to the rostrum with the bei mir waltz.

After a year's absence, and rest, the favourite opera returned to Covent Garden to open the 1927 season with the same principals as before. 'Bruno Walter, delightfully punctual, entered the orchestra pit at 7.15' (*Morning Post*), and Act I was broadcast 'over all stations by wireless—2LO and 5XX Daventry' (*The Times*). The performance received a 'rave' notice, and 'ripples of laughter were heard here and there which had not been there before'.

The *Morning Post* (Francis Toye) said that with the three principal ladies the 'lovely singing of the final duet and trio remains one of the most delightful operatic memories of our time'. And, 'Every actor could learn a useful lesson in dignity and repose from Lotte Lehmann's interpretation of the Feldmarschallin.'

Hermann Klein, in the *Gramophone* of June 1927, observed: 'The Baron Ochs of Richard Mayr . . . seemed once more to have been "resurrected" bodily from the naughty Vienna of 1750.'

Royal Opera House, Covent Garden
April 22, 1929, for five performances in German

	April 22, 1929	April 25, 1929	May 1, 1929	May 14, 1929	May 17, 1929
Octavian	Reinhardt	Reinhardt	Reinhardt	Reinhardt	Reinhardt
Marschallin	Lehmann	Ohms	Leider	Lehmann	Lehmann
Baron Ochs	Mayr	Mayr	Mayr	Mayr	Mayr
Valzacchi	Reiss	Reiss	Reiss	Reiss	Reiss
Annina	Andrassy	Andrassy	Andrassy	Andrassy	Andrassy
Tenor Singer	F. Russell	F. Russell	F. Russell	F. Russell	F. Russell
von Faninal	Habich	Madin	Madin	Habich	Madin
Sophie	Alpar	Alpar	Alpar	Schumann	Schumann
Conductor	Walter	Heger	Heger	Walter	Walter

Scenery specially designed and painted by Ernest Woodroffe Millar
The Stage under the direction of Charles Moor

The 1929 season opened with the opera once again, and to the usual packed house. There was, however, a new Sophie in the Hungarian soprano Gita Alpar, whose situation in following Elisabeth Schumann was not to be envied. She was 'an accomplished artist with a voice of brilliant quality which told very effectively in the love music of the second act' (*The Times*). But she could not quite compare with Schumann, who returned for the last two performances to make up the standard cast again, and for the last time. May 17 was Delia Reinhardt's final appearance at Covent Garden.

Meanwhile the Dutch soprano, Elisabeth Ohms, was the new Marschallin at the second performance—the only time she ever sang the part in London. Mme. Ohms was better known here as Brünnhilde and Isolde, but two gramophone records testify to her deeply felt and beautifully sung Princess of Werdenberg.

Mme. Frida Leider sung the Marschallin at the third *Rosenkavalier* on May 1, for the first time in London.

Among the smaller parts, Eduard Habich was singled out for praise as the 'pompous Faninal', and Anny Andrassy was much liked as the new Annina.

Robert Heger shared the conducting with Bruno Walter.

Royal Opera House, Covent Garden
April 27, 1931, for four performances in German

	April 27, 1931	*May 1, 1931*	*May 7, 1931*	*May 12, 1931*
Octavian	Angerer	Angerer	Angerer	Olczewska
Marschallin	Lehmann	Lehmann	Leider	Leider
Baron Ochs	Mayr	Mayr	Mayr	Mayr
Valzacchi	Tessmer	Tessmer	Tessmer	Tessmer
Annina	Tibell	Tibell	Tibell	Tibell
Tenor Singer	Nash	Nash	Nash	Nash
von Faninal	Habich	Habich	Habich	Habich
Sophie	Schumann	Schumann	Schumann	Schumann
Conductor	Walter	Heger	Heger	Heger

Scenery specially designed and painted by Ernest Woodroffe Millar
The Stage under the direction of Charles Moor

The 'established opener' of the season was a jubilant performance, but regrettably it was to be Bruno Walter's last. A new Octavian, Margit Angerer (Hungarian and leading soprano at Vienna since 1927) did not receive as much acclaim as Reinhardt had done. Already a new order was creeping in and *Rosenkavalier* fanciers were beginning to shake their heads and hark back. Mayr's Ochs continued in its perfection of 'a unique character' but this was, alas, his last season in London, too, although he lived for another four years. *The Times* found the 'ensembles clear in detail and nothing more enjoyable than the *delicate*[1] scherzo opening to the last act'.

The *Daily Mail* found Lehmann and Mayr 'unsurpassable' and Angerer 'as pretty as a piece of Dresden China but too feminine to make the boy'. Her voice was considered 'perhaps more Mozartian than Straussian'. Bruno Walter and the LSO gave a 'lighter and less exuberant' performance than hitherto.

The *Daily Telegraph* noted various changes in the production, particularly in the opening of the first act. Mayr's voice was thought to have lost something of its resonance but he acted wonderfully, especially in Act III.

Heger conducted the last three performances, and was beginning to emerge as a popular figure on the rostrum. Heddle Nash scored with the tenor aria and was applauded.

[1] Author's italics.

Covent Garden Opera Touring Company, Autumn 1931

When Lt.-Col. Blois became Managing Director of the Covent Garden Opera Syndicate in 1925, he was found to have sympathies with British singers. When the British National Opera Company could no longer carry on in 1929 Blois made them the Covent Garden Opera Touring Company, and for three years they travelled the provinces in the winter and spring of each year.

Theatre Royal, Glasgow
October 29, November 2, 1931
  Rosenkavalier in English

King's Theatre, Edinburgh
November 10, 20, 1931
  Rosenkavalier in English

Empire Theatre, Liverpool
November 23, December 1, 1931
  Rosenkavalier in English

Prince of Wales Theatre, Birmingham
December 7, 15, 1931
  Rosenkavalier in English

Cast for all eight performances

Octavian	Parry
Marschallin	Licette
Baron Ochs	Allin
Valzacchi	Davies
Annina	Parr
Tenor Singer	H. Tree
von Faninal	Michael
Sophie	Gruhn
Conductor	Barbirolli

New settings were made for this tour and the opera was produced afresh.

In Edinburgh 'the performance masterly in clearness and vivacity'; Ochs a 'Viennese Falstaff'.

In Liverpool Licette 'brilliant' and the audience recalled the days of the Denhof Tour.

Covent Garden Opera Touring Company, Spring 1932

Streatham Hill Theatre, London
January 25, 30 (mat.), February 5, 1932
Rosenkavalier in English

Hippodrome, Golders Green, London
February 8, 16, 18 (*mat.*), 1932
Rosenkavalier in English

Theatre Royal, Halifax
February 22, 24 (*mat.*), March 2, 1932
Rosenkavalier in English

Opera House, Manchester
March 7, 12 (*mat.*), 15, 1932
Rosenkavalier in English

Cast for all twelve performances:

Octavian	Parry
Marschallin	Licette
Baron Ochs	Allin
Valzacchi	Davies
Annina	Parr
Tenor Singer	H. Tree
von Faninal	Michael
Sophie	Gruhn
Conductor	Barbirolli

At Streatham Hill—'this felicitous English version by Alfred Kalisch'—the January 25 performance was the first one in London in English. The *Daily Mail* said that 'Norman Allin played Ochs quite in the grand manner with great richness and the right rude fun'. The production followed familiar lines and the costumes were sufficiently resplendent. But something of the lingering bitter-sweetness was lost which the slower tempo of German allows. 'Mr. Barbirolli does wonderful things with an orchestra of fifty.'

Covent Garden Opera Touring Company, Autumn 1932

Theatre Royal, Glasgow
October 24, November 12, 1932
Rosenkavalier in English

King's Theatre, Edinburgh
November 10, 18, 1932
Rosenkavalier in English

Theatre Royal, Halifax
November 25, December 1, 1932
  Rosenkavalier in English

Opera House, Manchester
December 8, 1932
  Rosenkavalier in English

Cast for all seven performances:

Octavian	Parry
Marschallin	Licette
Baron Ochs	Allin
Valzacchi	Davies
Annina	Parr
Tenor Singer	H. Tree
von Faninal	Michael
Sophie	Lemmon
Conductor	Barbirolli

The appointment of Beecham as chief conductor at Covent Garden for the 1933 season was a result of opera politics and the withdrawal of the subsidy which the BBC had given to the Opera House for the past three years. Lt.-Col. Blois was ill (he died on May 16) and the season opened 'and was played out in an atmosphere of sadness and uncertainty'.[1]

Royal Opera House, Covent Garden
May 1, 4, 9, 1933, for three performances in German

Octavian	Hadrabova
Marschallin	Lehmann
Baron Ochs	Kipnis
Valzacchi	Fleischer
Annina	Parr
Tenor Singer	Nash
von Faninal	Habich
Sophie	Kern
Conductor	Beecham

Designer not stated

At the opening performance of the season 'Sir Thomas Beecham received more than the customary compliment by way of applause' (*The Times*). 'Sweet Lotte Lehmann has survived that we can hardly think of *Rosenkavalier* without her', said the *Daily Telegraph*, who also

[1] *Rosenthal*, p. 481.

found that this was far from that 'faultless cast of bygone *Rosenkavaliers*, that is, of the first Beecham production or the 1924 revival'. Neville Cardus in the *Manchester Guardian* found Mme. Lehmann 'less confident in difficult parts'. Heddle Nash as the Singer again found favour. Eva Hadrabova, the Octavian, a part which she had sung in Berlin and Salzburg, was thought by *The Times* to be ill at ease, not aristocratic enough and 'better as the hoyden in Act III' than as the boy. The *Daily Telegraph* found it disconcerting that Hadrabova 'surely the tallest Rose Cavalier' should be cast opposite 'the shortest Sophie ever seen'. This was Adele Kern, whose head came well below Hadrabova's shoulders 'in their glittering white satin embrace of Act II. Neither has yet a finished style of singing', said this critic.

The Ochs of Alexander Kipnis could not stand up to Mayr's interpretation, for so long and so recently remembered. Kipnis's personality (said the *Morning Post*) 'is not in reality funny in itself. If he wanted to make a point he inclined to buffoonery.'

It was generally agreed that the ensembles were well studied and performed, and Beecham's outstanding feature was clarity. The *Morning Post* said that 'the plasticity and *enchaînement* of rhythms were remarkable. The Viennese lusciousness was not stressed, thus giving the music a new purity.'

In his notice for the *Manchester Guardian* Neville Cardus criticised Sir Thomas for the 'unintelligent' cuts in the first act, which deprived Baron Ochs of the opportunity of uttering those outbursts which made the Marschallin eventually despise him. Beecham replied in another newspaper (the *Daily Telegraph*) and withdrew Neville Cardus's tickets for the whole season. The incident is described by Mr. Cardus in his biography of Beecham.[1]

Strauss says himself,[2] 'it is not true that a well-composed and dramatically carefully arranged opera is made shorter by cuts'. It depends where they are made and how they are made to effect better proportions and distribution of light and shade. Some of the Dresden elisions annoyed Strauss so much that he wrote to the musical director saying that he had forgotten one important cut; 'the trio in the third act only impeded the action, and I suggested the following cuts: D major: "Ich weiss nix, garnix" to G major: beginning of the last duet. . . .'[3]

Royal Opera House, Covent Garden

June 1, 1936, for three performances in German

	June 1, 9, 1936	*June 3, 1936*
Octavian	Lemnitz	Lemnitz
Marschallin	Rethberg	Rethberg
Baron Ochs	List	List
Valzacchi	Fleischer	Fleischer
Annina	M. Booth	Parr

[1] Neville Cardus, *Sir Thomas Beecham*, 1961, pp. 35–36 and p. 99.
[2] *Recollections*, pp. 158–9.
[3] *Ibid.*

	June 1, 9, 1936	June 3, 1936
Tenor Singer	Nash	Nash
von Faninal	Neumann	Neumann
Sophie	Andreva	Andreva
Conductor	Reiner	Reiner

New Scenery for Acts I and II designed by Nina Tokumbet

Producer not stated

Once again this opera graced the season, but 'the whole performance was, with the exception of Lemnitz, a far cry from the great evenings under Walter in the twenties' (*The Times*). There was new scenery, designed by Mme. Nina Tokumbet, which added freshness to the first two acts but did not depart in plan from that formerly in use.

The Times considered that Rethberg's 'voice has the richness which readily softens to pathos so that her change from rapture in the opening scene to the reflection . . . gives the measure of the Marschallin's character and place in the drama'.

'Tiana Lemnitz as Octavian was less boisterous than some have been. She is a true and fine artist'—the same paper continued. Ernest Newman, in the *Sunday Times*, had more to say about Lemnitz's performance. 'She showed us four Octavians: the boy of the first half of the first act; the very different boy of the second act; and the two quite different creations of the boy masquerading as the girl in the third act and in the second half of the first act. All these have to be distinguished yet all recognisable . . . as variations of a single personality. Here is a woman playing the part of a boy who is playing the part of a woman.'

As Ochs, Emmanuel List gave 'little singing, and it is singing which can redeem the part from vulgarity', said *The Times*. Once more Heddle Nash's performance of the tenor aria was praised—'it was consummate legato singing'.

The conductor Reiner came from the U.S.A. Originally Knappertsbusch was invited to conduct *Rosenkavalier* but, owing to his unpopularity with the Nazis, he was not given permission to leave Germany.

The *Daily Telegraph* called the performance '*Rosenkavalier* with a difference . . .; what of the 1936 vintage from this celebrated cru?' it asked; and answered, 'Not supremely memorable.'

Royal Opera House, Covent Garden
Visit of Dresden State Opera
November 2, 1936, for two performances in German

	November 2, 1936	November 10, 1936
Octavian	Rohs	Wieber
Marschallin	Fuchs	Fuchs
Baron Ochs	Ermold*	Ermold

* Ludwig Ermold sung the small part of the Notary in the first production of the opera at Dresden in 1911

	November 2, 1936	November 10, 1936
Valzacchi	H. Lange	H. Lange
Annina	Jung	Jung
Tenor Singer	Kremer	Kremer
von Faninal	Schellenberg	Schellenberg
Sophie	Cebotari	Cebotari
Conductor	Böhm	Böhm

Scenery and Costumes designed by Professor A. Roller and Adolf Mahnke
Producer Hans Strohbach

Apart from the 1924 production of *Rosenkavalier* which had a distinct sprinkling of Viennese singers, nothing as unified as the 1936 Dresden performances had ever been seen at Covent Garden. The critics tended to preach to the administration and to the public, especially Ernest Newman, who wrote something approaching a manifesto.

The main shock which everyone enjoyed was the realisation that 'everything in the Dresden performances' (and this applied to their repertoire)[1] 'settings, costumes, action, unified down to the smallest detail, achieved a product that was an organic unity from head to foot'.

The Dresden Company's visit probably did more for opera in London 'now that production is the magic word' than anything or anyone else, up to the production of *Don Carlos* by Visconti, twenty-two years later.

The Dresden Company proved that their roots were deep by using the original 1911 sets. W. J. Turner, in the *Illustrated London News*, gives the best, concise account: '*Rosenkavalier* was given an excellent performance by a cast which was an extremely good all-round one. The excellent teamwork was a feature throughout. The Octavian (Marta Rohs) was one of the best we have ever had at Covent Garden, and the Sophie of Maria Cebotari was quite the best I have ever heard here. She has a delightful voice and fine presence and sings with great charm. The Baron Ochs of Ludwig Ermold was a most effective representation of the part, and in spite of the fact that he gave us far more real singing than others have in this role, yet he was equally successful in bringing out the broad farcical effects of Acts II and III. The Marschallin of Marta Fuchs was a rendering in every way in keeping with its character— dignified, gracious and with that slight suggestion of approaching middle age, which is needed.'

'The weak spot in the cast was Arno Schellenberg's von Faninal, which was too youthful and insufficiently bourgeois.' This adverse criticism by Ernest Newman was the only one offered among a welter of praise and admiration. The same critic ended by asking how Covent Garden could ever hope to achieve anything like the standard of the Dresden Company when we obtain 'a heterogeneous collection of singers from this and that opera house, even from no opera house at all'.

[1] They brought *Rosenkavalier, Tristan und Isolde, Don Juan (Don Giovanni* in German), *Figaros Hochzeit* and *Ariadne II.*

Royal Opera House, Covent Garden
May 4, 1938, for four performances in German

	May 4, 1938	May 10, 12, 1938	May 23, 1938
Octavian	Lemnitz	Lemnitz	Lemnitz
Marschallin	{ Lehmann Konetzni	Lehmann	Konetzni
Baron Ochs	Krenn	Krenn	Krenn
Valzacchi	Tessmer	Tessmer	Laufkötter
Annina	Schilp	Schilp	Schilp
Tenor Singer	W. Booth	W. Booth	W. Booth
von Faninal	Habich	Habich	Wiedermann
Sophie	Berger	Berger	Beilke
Conductor	Kleiber	Kleiber	Zweig

Designer not stated   Producer and Stage Director: Charles Moor

The return of Lotte Lehmann to London in her part of the Marschallin was an event which was awaited with special interest. Although it was five years since Mme. Lehmann had sung this part at Covent Garden, there had been only two productions of *Rosenkavalier* without her—one of them by the visiting Dresden Company. So it was not as if an annual parade of less familiar Marschallins had passed by.

Nevertheless this was to be Mme. Lehmann's last season at the Opera House, and in an opera which suffered from ill-fortune throughout the season.

The grip of the Nazis on Germany and on Europe was making itself felt. A number of the singers who came to Covent Garden were ardent supporters of Hitler—others, like Kleiber (who was forbidden to conduct in Germany and Austria), and Mme. Lehmann, were not only opposed to the régime, but were anxious for the safety of their families and friends. In this atmosphere of oppression, and immediately after a bad five-day voyage from America, Mme. Lehmann started the first act of *Rosenkavalier* on May 4, and sung with some signs of distress as far as the end of the levée. Not only the audience in the Opera House, but thousands of listeners to the BBC's National programme, heard Mme. Lehmann gasp, and mutter a few words: 'I can't go on . . . finish.' There was a swish as the curtains closed, and then the audience broke into gasps of surprise. By great good fortune Hilde Konetzni was in front, and offered to take over at once. While she was changing and the costume was being altered to fit her ampler figure, the audience had an extra interval, while the broadcast was suspended, not to be resumed.

Mme. Konetzni had sung the part of the Marschallin under Kleiber before, so musically she was assured; but she had never sung in the London production. It was the gesture of a 'trouper' to take over without rehearsal.

On the next morning Covent Garden issued the following statement:

'Mme. Lotte Lehmann felt ill and saw that it was impossible for her to sing the end of the act to the audience's and her own satisfaction.

'Mme. Hilde Konetzni, who was present in the audience, was appealed to by the management and at once consented to take up the part which she has often sung under the direction of Herr Erich Kleiber, tonight's conductor, at Vienna, Prague, etc. She changed hurriedly and the first act was resumed from the point where it was broken off.'

A specialist who examined Mme. Lehmann said she had a chill and he advised her not to continue. He said she would be quite well again in a few days.

Hilde Konetzni 'sang magnificently', saved the performance, and was supported by Lemnitz as Octavian, the gloriously youthful voice of Berger's Sophie and the 'new and thoroughly convincing Ochs' of Fritz Krenn. (Prohaska had been announced for the part.) Kleiber, conducting for the first time at the Opera House, proved himself to be an opera conductor 'of the first water' as Ernest Newman put it. He was well remembered twelve years later.

Rosenkavalier was due for a repetition on May 11, but audiences who arrived on the 10th expecting to hear *Die Entführung* found *Rosenkavalier* on the bill instead, and their programmes slipped as follows:

NOTICE

Owing to the sudden indisposition of RICHARD TAUBER "DER ROSENKAVALIER" will be performed tonight instead of "DIE ENTFUHRUNG AUS DEM SERIAL". Madame LOTTE LEHMANN has consented to sing, and Mmes. TIANA LEMNITZ and MARIA LUISE SCHILP have flown from the Continent to complete the cast.

Lotte Lehmann was able to sing and vindicated herself nobly. Two days later, on May 12, she sang for the last time in London, and left at once to join her sick husband, having obtained Beecham's reluctant permission. The last *Rosenkavalier* on May 29 had Konetzni once more deputising for Lehmann, and with a new and charming Sophie in Beilke, and a satisfactory Faninal sung by Wiedemann. The performance was conducted by Fritz Zweig, already a refugee from Nazi-ism.

So ended the series of thirty-seven between-war performances of *Der Rosenkavalier* at Covent Garden in twenty-five of which Lotte Lehmann sang the Marschallin. No wonder that she should be so intimately associated with the part, and that with her retirement in 1938 an operatic era had ended.

Sadler's Wells Theatre, London
March 8, 1939, for seven performances in English

	March 8, 11, 1939	*March 17, 1939*	*April 1, 11, 1939*	*April 26, May 9, 1939*
Octavian	McArden	McArden	McArden	McArden
Marschallin	Cross	Cross	Cross	Cross

	March 8, 11, 1939	March 17, 1939	April 11, 1939	April 26, May 9, 1939
Baron Ochs	Stear	Stear	Stear	Stear
Valzacchi	M. Jones	M. Jones	M. Jones	M. Jones
Annina	Iacopi	Iacopi	Iacopi	Iacopi
Tenor Singer	W. Booth	W. Booth	W. Booth	H. Tree
van Faninal	Llewellyn	Dowling	Llewellyn	Llewellyn
Sophie	Naylor	Naylor	Naylor	Naylor
Conductor	Collingwood	Collingwood	Collingwood	Collingwood

Scenery, costumes and furniture designed by Hamish Wilson
Scenery for Act I painted by George Wiggins
Scenery for Acts II and III painted by Edward Delaney
Producer: Clive Carey

In 1939 at Sadler's Wells *Der Rosenkavalier* emerged unexpectedly in an English guise and in a production which delighted all who attended it.

Lilian Bayliss invited Richard Strauss to attend the opening performance and he replied by telegram: 'I rejoice to hear that *Rosenkavalier* is to be given in English at Sadler's Wells, and I send my best wishes for its success. My doctor will not let me come North until April, so I regret I cannot accept your kind invitation to be present.'[1]

The *Daily Telegraph* recalled that the opera had been heard in English at Streatham Hill Theatre for one production in 1932 (see p. 81); *The Times* advised its readers to accustom themselves 'to the English title since last night's production at Sadler's Wells showed that what has so long been known at Covent Garden as *Der Rosenkavalier* is to take a permanent place in the English repertory. Presumably the text is by Kalisch and is what was used by the Denhof Company. . . .'

The Times went on to say that the text was hardly heard and some of the singers were mainly inaudible; but the excellence of the sets and costumes, and 'the care which Mr. Clive Carey had expended on the groupings of crowd scenes' as well as the 'performance of some of the leading singers, showed that *The Rosebearer* has now come to stay'.

The *Daily Telegraph*, recalling the early thirties when Norman Allin and Agnes Nicholls sang Ochs and the Marschallin respectively, found that Sadler's Wells had not quite another Allin, but 'Joan Cross is distinguished enough to justify the enterprise . . . an exquisite performance, the crown of her career'. Ruth Naylor's Sophie was 'charming' and 'an achievement'. Joy McArden was 'bright voiced', Webster Booth 'sung the Italian song beautifully' and Valetta Iacopi was 'very good as Annina'. Only Ronald Stear's Ochs did not come up to the standard of the rest of the cast, he 'did not seem to have made up his mind how far to carry the low comedy of the part, and allowed Act III to lose a good deal of its point with Joy McArden . . .' (*The Times*).

It was noted that the usual cuts were made in the part of Baron Ochs in Act I, and that von Hofmannsthal's name did not appear anywhere on the programme.

[1] Strauss was at this time working on the score of *Die Liebe der Danae*.

The designer of the opera, Hamish Wilson, had conceived the excellent (though somewhat filmic) idea of presenting the white and silver-clad lovers in the second act upon a black floor which would shine and reflect their brightness in it. He had ordered a large expanse of American cloth to cover the acting area, and this arrived at the theatre on the day before the first performance. Apart from the fact that the shiny surface would also reflect the stage lights above it, the L.C.C.'s fire regulations do not allow the use of such material. Rather than face a last minute rejection by the inspector on the first night, and the possible stopping of the show, the authorities were called in by the desperate stage manager, Henry Robinson, and a catastrophe averted. All were satisfied when an ordinary black stage-cloth was put down to replace the highly inflammable one.

Royal Opera House, Covent Garden
1947 Season
April 22, 1947, for ten performances in English

	April 22, 25, 28, May 1, 9, 13, 20, 30, 1947	June 27, July 5, 1947
Octavian	Sladen	Sladen
Marschallin	Doree	Doree
Baron Ochs	Franklin	Franklin
Valzacchi	Norville	Norville
Annina	Shacklock	Shacklock
Tenor Singer	Neate	Neate
von Faninal	Clifford	Clifford
Sophie	MacWatters	Lynn
Conductor	Rankl	Rankl

Designer: Robin Ironside   Producer: Joan Cross

'Here it is again,' said *The Times*, 'with new singers in a changed world.' Gone was the glory of the old International Summer Season indeed, but here was a *Rosenkavalier* with an almost entirely English cast, as one of a slender repertoire of six operas—two German, two French and two Italian—in the national Opera House. The new translation was by Alan Pryce-Jones.

It was partly due to the musical director, Karl Rankl, that this opera was mounted and was the fourth to be produced in the first season. It was very much more to Rankl's temperament than had been *Carmen* or *Zauberflöte*, and was more successful than either of these.

The producer, Joan Cross, who had been London's last pre-war Marschallin at Sadler's Wells, made a thorough and intelligent job of it. The sets by Robin Ironside [1] were practical if undistinguished, although it seemed ill-considered that the traditional Lerchenau colours of green and white should be pervading the Marschallin's boudoir.

[1] These were still in use, with some modifications, up to Spring 1963.

David Franklin's Baron Ochs was in no way Austrian, was too young and refined, but excellent in articulation and with 'euphonious, agreeable singing'. Graham Clifford's characterisation and singing of Faninal was disliked. The other major parts were taken well; Doris Doree as the Marschallin was described by *The Times* as 'a really splendid Princess who is treasure trove from America'; while Victoria Sladen's accomplished Octavian 'represents the heady emotion of youth . . . in voice and gait and gesture and appearance'.

The first two Sophies of the production were undistinguished (particularly Leni Lynn who had never sung in opera before); but the tenor singer, Kenneth Neate, gave a truly Italian flavour to his aria.

The Times stated equivocally: 'The revival is a credit to all at Covent Garden. Living in an impoverished world, we drink in the extravagant and gorgeous sounds with nostalgic relish —and disgust.'

The performance on May 9 passed unnoticed as the fiftieth *Rosenkavalier* at Covent Garden.

Covent Garden Opera, Provincial Tour 1947

The first post-war opera season by the new Company had ended with their tenth perform-ance of *Rosenkavalier* on July 5, 1947. After an interval of six weeks, the first tour started. The full repertorie of six operas [1] was taken to four cities and to Croydon, playing a fortnight in each. That this tour should have been planned and executed so early in the life of the young Opera Company was no doubt due to a need to 'show the flag'. Certainly some provincial taxpayers appreciated this proof that their contributions were not being spent solely for the benefit of metropolitan audiences.

Theatre Royal, Glasgow
August 26, 1947, for two performances in English

	August 26, 1947	*August 28, 1947*
Octavian	Sladen	Sladen
Marschallin	Doree	Doree
Baron Ochs	Franklin	Franklin
Valzacchi	Norville	Norville
Annina	Shacklock	Shacklock
Tenor Singer	Edgar Evans	Edgar Evans
von Faninal	Clifford	Clifford
Sophie	Lynn	Turner
Conductor	Rankl	Rankl

Designer: Robin Ironside

Producer: Joan Cross

[1] *Carmen, The Magic Flute, Manon* (Massenet), *Il Trovatore* and *Turandot*, all in English, were the others.

Of the first of these performances the *Glasgow Herald* said: 'Glasgow is grateful to the Covent Garden Opera Company for . . . bringing with them such fine revivals. The last of these, *Rosenkavalier*, was staged last night in the Theatre Royal. Praise must be given to the settings and great commendation goes to Karl Rankl for his splendid handling of the orchestra.'

Empire Theatre, Liverpool
September 3, 11, 1947, in English

Opera House, Manchester
September 19, 24, 1947, in English

Theatre Royal, Birmingham
September 30,[1] 1947, in English

Davis Theatre, Croydon
October 17, 23, 1947, in English

Cast for all seven performances:

Octavian	Sladen
Marschallin	Doree
Baron Ochs	Franklin
Valzacchi	Norville
Annina	Shacklock
Tenor Singer	Edgar Evans
von Faninal	Clifford
Sophie	Lynn
Conductor	Rankl

Designer: Robin Ironside   Producer: Joan Cross

The *Manchester Evening News* observed: 'If the half dozen works . . . given us have included nothing strange or rare, that is excusable at this particular time, when the directorate is just beginning to build up what the war cast down. . . . The same reason is behind the lack of real quality of much of the singing, in which it is not difficult to discern faults.'

This kind of criticism—however valid—was not apparent elsewhere. The *Birmingham Post and Mail* gave enthusiastic notices. The *Croydon Advertiser* ended by saying: 'Karl Rankl conducted an orchestra that flashed and shimmered with the lively and passionate score. . . . It was indeed a triumphant occasion.'

[1] **Walter Midgley** was shown in the programme as the Tenor Singer, but Edgar Evans appeared as usual.

Royal Opera House, Covent Garden
1947/48 Season
November 1, 1948, for six performances in English

	November 1, December 2, 19, 1947	January 15, 1948	February 17, 1948	May 19, 1948
Octavian	Sladen	Sladen	Sladen	Sladen
Marschallin	Doree	Abercrombie	Doree	Doree
Baron Ochs	Franklin	Franklin	Franklin	Franklin
Valzacchi	Norville	Norville	Norville	Norville
Annina	Shacklock	Shacklock	Shacklock	Shacklock
Tenor Singer	Neate	Neate	Neate	Neate
von Faninal	Clifford	Clifford	Clifford	Clifford
Sophie	Lynn	Lynn	Schwarzkopf	Schwarzkopf
Conductor	Rankl	Rankl	Rankl	Gellhorn

Designer: Robin Ironside   Producer: Joan Cross

The new season's cast for the first three *Rosenkavaliers* was identical to the last performance of the previous production. These were followed in the bitter January of 1948—when the Opera House's heating arrangements were perforce at a low thermal level—by an understudy Marschallin.

But a new Sophie on February 17 raised the standard of the production considerably. As *The Times* said, '*Rosenkavalier* was on the whole the best of the first batch of productions by the Covent Garden Opera Company in its first year. With the return of Miss Doree and the temporary accession of Mme. Schwarzkopf, the opera in its present revival has an added depth and a greater finish. . . .' Mme. Schwarzkopf's 'sure high notes now put the final touch of beauty to the concerted music . . . [and] . . . her characterization is dramatically true in that she conveys in succession the ingenuousness, the spirit, and the sweetness of the girl'. David Franklin's Ochs was thought to have improved and 'carries complete conviction'. The *Daily Telegraph*, in praising Mme. Schwarzkopf and Victorian Sladen, felt that 'the duets in Act II rose well above the average, in a production well meaning rather than well-bred'.

Royal Opera House, Covent Garden
1948/49 Season
October 1, 1948, for four performances in English

	October 1, 1948	October 28, 1948	November 24, 1948	February 9, 1949
Octavian	Shacklock	Shacklock	Shacklock	Shacklock
Marschallin	Doree	Doree	Doree	Abercrombie
Baron Ochs	Franklin	Franklin	Franklin	Franklin
Valzacchi	Norville	Norville	Norville	Norville

	October 1, 1948	October 28, 1948	November 28, 1948	February 9, 1949
Annina	Francis-Sirou	Francis-Sirou	Francis-Sirou	Francis-Sirou
Tenor Singer	Neate	Schock	Schock	Schock
von Faninal	Clifford	Clifford	Clifford	Clifford
Sophie	Schwarzkopf	S. Russell	S. Russell	S. Russell
Conductor	Rankl	Rankl	Gellhorn	Rankl

Designer: Robin Ironside   Producer: Joan Cross

It was becoming clear that repetition had greatly improved the standard of performances dramatically, musically and in the progress of characterisation. Doree's Marschallin, Franklin's Ochs and Rankl's handling of orchestra and singers had all taken forward strides. In particular it was noted by the Earl of Harewood in *Ballet and Opera*[1] that 'Dr. Rankl is now able to concentrate his gifts as interpreter as opposed to teacher, to the definite benefit of the performance'.

The American soprano Shirley Russell was the new Sophie after the first performance of the season, and made an unqualified success. The voice was beautiful and pure and her acting was right for the ingénue part. Constance Shacklock as Octavian was thought to be 'musically well on the way to distinction' (*The Times*). She was to be the resident Octavian for the next eleven years, adding all the time to this, her best role.

Royal Opera House, Covent Garden
1949/50 Season
October 28, 1949, for five performances in English

	October 28, 1949	November 15, 1949	December 10, 1949	December 20, 1949	May 9, 1949
Octavian	Shacklock	Shacklock	Shacklock	Shacklock	Shacklock
Marschallin	Fisher	Fisher	Fisher	Doree	Fisher
Baron Ochs	Glynne	Glynne	Glynne	Franklin	Glynne
Valzacchi	P. Jones	P. Jones	P. Jones	P. Jones	P. Jones
Annina	J. Watson	J. Watson	J. Watson	J. Watson	J. Watson
Tenor Singer	Neate	Dickie	Schock	Neate	Schock
von Faninal	Clifford	Clifford	Clifford	Clifford	Ronald Lewis
Sophie	Berger	Schwarzkopf	Schwarzkopf	Loose	Schwarzkopf
Conductor	Rankl	Gellhorn	Rankl	Rankl	Rankl

The Australian soprano, Sylvia Fisher, who had made her début on the opera stage three weeks before as Leonore in *Fidelio*, was to prove a valuable addition to the permanent Company for the next eight years. She grew slowly into the character of the Marschallin—as is only to be expected—and in this first season showed little indication of the maturity which she was later to give to the part.

[1] November 1948, p. 52.

93

Howell Glynne was a Welsh Ochs and failed to portray von Hofmannsthal's razor-edge, ambiguous creation.

On the whole, the production had not improved and the orchestra played heavily and with frequent ugly sounds.

On December 20, Emmy Loose from Vienna gave something of the spirit of that city to her performance and was thought to be the best post-war interpreter of Sophie.

At the last performance of the season, Ronald Lewis, a baritone who was beginning to emerge from the chorus as a singer of small parts, took over von Faninal from Clifford. Lewis was soon to make this part his own in both English and German performances and for many years to come. Doree returned to sing the Marschallin and Parry Jones was praised for the attention he gave to the part of Valzacchi.

Royal Opera House, Covent Garden
1950/51 Season
November 4, 1950, for eight performances in English

	November 4, 1950	November 23, 1950	December 6, 1950	December 15, 1950	January 4, 20, February 9, 22, 1951
Octavian	Shacklock	Shacklock	Shacklock	Shacklock	Shacklock
Marschallin	Fisher	Fisher	Fisher	Fisher	Fisher
Baron Ochs	Glynne	Glynne	Glynne	Glynne	Glynne
Valzacchi	P. Jones	P. Jones	P. Jones	P. Jones	P. Jones
Annina	J. Watson	J. Watson	J. Watson	J. Watson	J. Watson
Tenor Singer	Dickie	Johnston	Johnston	Dickie	Johnston
von Faninal	Clifford	Clifford	Clifford	Clifford	Clifford
Sophie	Schwarzkopf	Schwarzkopf	Graf	Graf	Graf
Conductor	Rankl	Rankl	Kleiber	Kleiber	Kleiber

Designer: Robin Ironside — Producer not stated

'The human warmth of Strauss's score can raise a fellow-feeling, sometimes to the point of tears, in a performance of *Rosenkavalier*, even when the Company is not stylistically at one in its approach to the opera,' said *The Times*. This half-compliment was amplified by appreciation of the 'beautifully blended trio of Miss Fisher, Mme. Schwarzkopf and Miss Shacklock. Each has her triumphs.' These were: for Sylvia Fisher 'in the closing pages of the first act when the beauty of her tone can efface the memory of more celebrated Marschallins', and for Schwarzkopf and Shacklock 'in the presentation scene and the duet that followed it'. Glynne, on the other hand, was criticised for making Ochs a character of 'easy-going lechery' rather than a representative of 'debauched aristocracy'.

On December 6 Erich Kleiber began to assist in the forging of the Covent Garden Opera Company. *The Times* said: 'The performance proved to be a good omen, for it was the best yet given of this opera by this Company.' Both Shacklock and Glynne had improved their performances considerably, and, apart from Kleiber, the only newcomer to the cast was Uta Graf. This German soprano (from the San Francisco Opera Company) had a light voice that blended so well with Fisher's and Shacklock's that the greatest climax of a wonderfully musical evening was the third act trio. Thanks to Kleiber's magic with the orchestra, he 'caused the whole company to sing with their hearts'.

Covent Garden Opera Provincial Tour, March 1951

A provincial tour lasting only two weeks went out over Easter 1951. The first city visited was Edinburgh (where *Rosenkavalier* had not been heard since 1932), and the second was Manchester.

Empire Theatre, Edinburgh
March 17, 1951, for one performance in English

Palace Theatre, Manchester
March 31, 1951, for one performance in English

Cast for both performances:

Octavian	Shacklock
Marschallin	Fisher
Baron Ochs	Glynne
Valzacchi	P. Jones
Annina	J. Watson
Tenor Singer	Marlowe
von Faninal	Ronald Lewis
Sophie	Loose
Conductor	Gellhorn

Designer: Robin Ironside   Producer not stated

Covent Garden Opera Provincial Tour, July 1951

Grand, Leeds
July 11, 1951, for two performances in English

	July 11, 1951	July 16, 1951
Octavian	Shacklock	Shacklock
Marschallin	Fisher	Fisher
Baron Ochs	Glynne	Glynne
Valzacchi	D. Tree	P. Jones
Annina	J. Watson	J. Watson
Tenor Singer	Marlowe	Marlowe
von Faninal	Ronald Lewis	Ronald Lewis
Sophie	Berger	Berger
Conductor	Rankl	Gellhorn

Designer: Robin Ironside   Producer not stated

Rosenkavalier had not been heard in Leeds since 1913, when as *The Rose Bearer*, it was given a single performance at the same theatre by the Denhof Company.

Now, thirty-eight years later, the *Yorkshire Post* complimented the principals. Sylvia Fisher was 'a most sympathetic Princess, who sang throughout with purity and style'. Constance Shacklock was considered 'an excellent Octavian'. And of Howell Glynne this critic said 'he is very good. His admirable singing range leaves little to be desired.' And Dr. Rankl 'gave, for the most part, radiance and richness'.

Empire Theatre, Liverpool
July 27, 1951, for one performance in English

Octavian	Shacklock
Marschallin	Fisher
Baron Ochs	Glynne
Valzacchi	P. Jones
Annina	J. Watson
Tenor Singer	Marlowe
von Faninal	Ronald Lewis
Sophie	MacNeil
Conductor	Rankl

Designer: Robin Ironside   Producer not stated

The only unusual aspect of this performance was the Sophie of the American soprano Dorothy MacNeil. She had sung a good Cherubino and a poor Elvira at Glyndebourne before making this solitary appearance with the Covent Garden Company. She then returned to New York and has not sung again in Britain.

Royal Opera House, Covent Garden
1951/52 Season
December 28, 1951, for five performances in English

	December 28, 1951, January 3, 8, 16, 1952	*February 2, 1952*
Octavian	Shacklock	Shacklock
Marschallin	Fisher	Fisher
Baron Ochs	Glynne	Glynne
Valzacchi	P. Jones	P. Jones
Annina	J. Watson	J. Watson
Tenor Singer	Marlowe	Marlowe
von Faninal	Ronald Lewis	Ronald Lewis
Sophie	Guldbaek	Harvey
Conductor	Kleiber	Kleiber

Designer: Robin Ironside   Producer not stated

These performances achieved a high standard of excellence. 'The opera was extremely well cast,' said *The Times*, and went on: 'The new Sophie, Miss Ruth Guldbaek, who comes from Denmark, has a voice of singular purity, capable of warmth and animation which add charm to its sterling qualities of true intonation and firmness of line.' Praise also went to Fisher, whose interpretation of the Marschallin 'has ripened and is now most moving . . .'; Howell Glynne was thought to have 'gained in the dignity that it needs to present the aristocrat gone to seed . . . one can . . . begin to enjoy the characterization which formerly was out of his reach'.

Ronald Lewis was complimented on his Faninal, which he played 'without barking or fooling it and so gave us a convincing picture of the perplexed little man'.

Covent Garden Opera Provincial Tour, Spring 1952

Empire Theatre, Cardiff
February 26, 1952 (Welsh première of a Strauss opera) for one performance only, in English

Octavian	Shacklock
Marschallin	Fisher
Baron Ochs	Glynne
Valzacchi	P. Jones
Annina	J. Watson
Tenor Singer	Marlowe
von Faninal	Ronald Lewis
Sophie	Leigh
Conductor	Gellhorn

Designer: Robin Ironside   Producer not stated

Theatre Royal, Birmingham
April 3, 1952. One performance in English
  Cast as for Cardiff

Royal Opera House, Covent Garden
1951/52 Season
April 19, May 2, 29, 1952, for three performances in English

Octavian	Shacklock
Marschallin	Fisher
Baron Ochs	Glynne
Valzacchi	P. Jones
Annina	J. Watson
Tenor Singer	Marlowe
von Faninal	Ronald Lewis
Sophie	Leigh
Conductor	Gellhorn

Designer: Robin Ironside   Producer not stated

King's Theatre, Edinburgh
Edinburgh Festival 1952. Visit of Hamburg State Opera
August 28, 1952, for three performances in German

	August 28, 1952	August 30, 1952	September 5, 1952
Octavian	Mödl	Grümmer	Mödl
Marschallin	Ebers	Ebers	Ebers
Baron Ochs	Herrmann	Herrmann	Herrmann
Valzacchi	Göllnitz	Göllnitz	Göllnitz
Annina	Hedy Gura	Hedy Gura	Hedy Gura
Tenor Singer	Schock	Bensing	Lehnert
von Faninal	Bröcheler	Bröcheler	Bröcheler
Sophia	Della Casa	Della Casa	Della Casa
Conductor	Keilberth	Ludwig	Ludwig

Designer: Alfred Siercke   Producer: Günther Rennert

Edinburgh Festival audiences had become accustomed to the excellence of Carl Ebert's production of operas during past summers at the King's Theatre, and here was another in the same manner. 'Consistency is stressed, together with a thoroughly imaginative attention to detail . . . the eye was repeatedly caught by some nuance of behaviour, a shrug of the shoulders, a leer, a hesitation. . . . A spectacular climax of fuss and flurry was created during and after the duel in Act II, while the grand deception scene in the next act was carried out with full-blooded burlesque.' So said the *Scotsman*. This newspaper, in company with most others, gave credit to Theo Herrmann as Ochs and said, 'his performance dominated the whole opera. Full blown, ruffianly, and marvellously subtle, Ochs always managed to preserve his dignity even in the extremes of discomfiture.'

Of the ladies Clara Ebers was probably the least well cast. Eric Blom in the *Observer* felt that 'youthful, charming and talented [she] never suggested the great lady, the ageing woman or the oppression of luxurious indulgence . . .'. But this was perhaps too harsh a criticism as *Opera* found her 'well suited to the Marschallin'.[1]

Lisa Della Casa was described by Blom as 'an enchanting Sophie whose only slight fault was a tendency to hug her glorious high notes too affectionately'.

Martha Mödl, at the first and third performances, was said to have too round a tone to sound, and too ample a figure to appear boyish. At the second performance Elisabeth Grümmer as Octavian 'made a tall shapely boy and did some ravishingly beautiful singing during the course of the evening' (*Opera*)[2]. Von Faninal was cast to appear far more cultured than is usual, and as a result one could understand why the Act II sets had such charm.

Both sets for Acts II and III were outstandingly good. Due to the shallowness of the improvised, post-bombardment Hamburg stage (for which they were designed), the Act II

[1] Vol. III, No. 10, p. 588.
[2] *Ibid.*

98

staircase ran offstage on the O.P. side which made a pleasant change from the usual plan; and in Act III the set was divided to show both the room at the inn and a corridor beside it.

The Times noted that 'Unity of conception was again apparent and was responsible for raising a performance in which there were no stars to a high level of excellence notable for its concentration of the opera's peculiar bloom and fragrance.'

Royal Opera House, Covent Garden

1952/53 Season
October 29, November 7, 11, 1952, January 15, 1953, for four performances in English

Octavian	Shacklock
Marschallin	Fisher
Baron Ochs	Glynne
Valzacchi	Marlowe
Annina	Howitt
Tenor Singer	Asciak
von Faninal	Ronald Lewis
Sophie	Dunne
Conductor	Gellhorn

Designer: Robin Ironside   Producer not stated

Covent Garden Opera Provincial Tour, Spring 1953

King's Theatre, Glasgow
March 10, 1953, for one performance in English

Empire Theatre, Liverpool
March 20, 1953, for one performance in English

Palace Theatre, Manchester
March 26, 31, 1953, for two performances in English

Cast for all four performances:

Octavian	Shacklock
Marschallin	Fisher
Baron Ochs	Glynne
Valzacchi	Marlowe
Annina	Howitt
Tenor Singer	Asciak
von Faninal	Ronald Lewis
Sophie	Dunne
Conductor	Gellhorn

Designer: Robin Ironside   Producer not stated

99

Theatre Royal, Birmingham
April 9, 1953, for two performances in English

	April 9, 1953	*April 17, 1953*
Octavian	Shacklock	Shacklock
Marschallin	Fisher	Fisher
Baron Ochs	Glynne	Glynne
Valzacchi	Marlowe	Marlowe
Annina	Howitt	Howitt
Tenor Singer	Asciak	Asciak
von Faninal	Ronald Lewis	Ronald Lewis
Sophie	Leigh	Dunne
Conductor	Gellhorn	Gellhorn

Designer: Robin Ironside   Producer not stated

Royal Opera House, Covent Garden
1952/53 Season
April 24, 29, May 4, 9, 18, 29, 1953, for six performances in English

Octavian	Shacklock
Marschallin	Fisher
Baron Ochs	Glynne
Valzacchi	P. Jones
Annina	Howitt
Tenor Singer	Johnston
von Faninal	Ronald Lewis
Sophie	Leigh
Conductor	Kleiber

Designer: Robin Ironside   Producer not stated

Adèle Leigh came in for much criticism of her acting and singing of the part of Sophie, which was considered to be far too sophisticated and coquettish. Otherwise there was commendation for a production in which Kleiber alone was the guest. Kleiber was regarded as the supreme opera conductor to have visited Covent Garden since the war. *The Times* described his direction as 'a miracle of delicacy and discernment'. Cecil Smith said, 'The transformation of the orchestra was astounding . . . for any singer with a technique equal to Kleiber's expectations, it must be a joy to work with him. Every lyrical phrase was shaped with the utmost plasticity. A singer who failed to attain the maximum expressiveness could blame only himself, not the conductor. . . . The effect of Kleiber's inspired craftsmanship upon Sylvia Fisher was hardly less than marvellous.'

Miss Fisher had been improving on her interpretation all along but 'she has never touched the heights of her 1st Act performance as the Marschallin'. *The Times* considered that Fisher and Shacklock shared the honours on stage. 'Both had lived with the roles long enough to have discovered all their secrets and subtleties. . . .'

Howell Glynne sung and played an Ochs shorn of '. . . all trace of the plebeian and vulgar, and in his new restraint, with its suggestion of a former elegance, there is a pathos that wins far more sympathy for the old roué than ever before'.[1]

Cecil Smith finished his article: '. . . We did have Kleiber. We did have Fisher and Shacklock. We did have Robin Ironside's gay and pretty settings. Some day, maybe, we will also have a production.'

Royal Opera House, Covent Garden

1953/54 Season

July 20, 22, 24, 1954, for three performances in English

Octavian	Shacklock
Marschallin	Fisher
Baron Ochs	Dalberg
Valzacchi	Nilsson
Annina	Howitt
Tenor Singer	McAlpine
von Faninal	Ronald Lewis
Sophie	Guldbaek
Conductor	Kempe

Designer: Robin Ironside   Producer: Christopher West

After an absence of fourteen months the opera returned to Covent Garden under Rudolf Kempe's baton. London had heard the Bavarian State Opera meanwhile, and Kempe had been acquired from them as guest conductor.[1]

The standard cast of the last few years had a new Ochs in Dalberg, who was disappointing; a former Sophie returned in the person of Ruth Guldbaek (see 1951/52 Season); and a glorious new tenor singer: William McAlpine.

The first of these three performances, said Felix Aprahamian in the *Sunday Times*, 'confirmed his [Kempe's] prestige as a masterly conductor of Strauss operas.[2] This *Rosenkavalier* was complete—even to the restoration of a passage with which Strauss once declared himself unfamiliar—but Kempe's mercurial baton made the work sound swifter than usual'.[3]

Dalberg was playing Ochs for the first time but visualised it 'broadly—in the first act crudely, in fact—suggesting dissipation without any underlying dignity or good breeding' (*The Times*). Miss Guldbaek was not able to project the English words, though 'the purity of her tone and her shapely phrasing offered considerable compensation' (*The Times*).

At the last of the three performances (the last night of the 1953/54 Season), it would have seemed that there had been an attempt to improve the articulation of words. Sylvia Fisher

[1] *Opera* Vol. IV, No. 6, pp. 367-8.

[2] See p. 143.   [3] See p. 83 for Strauss's own views on cuts.

was praised for her continually moving interpretation and for her warm and round tone. So, too, was Constance Shacklock, for her 'delightfully eager, radiant characterization' (*The Times*).

Royal Opera House, Covent Garden
1954/55 Season
November 12, 1954 (100th performance of the opera at this House) for five performances in English

	November 12, 16, 27, 1954	November 29, December 2, 1954
Octavian	Shacklock	Shacklock
Marschallin	Fisher	Fisher
Baron Ochs	Dalberg	Glynne
Valzacchi	Nilsson	Nilsson
Annina	Howitt	Howitt
Tenor Singer	McAlpine	McAlpine
von Faninal	Ronald Lewis	Ronald Lewis
Sophie	Leigh	Leigh
Conductor	Kempe	Kempe

Designer: Robin Ironside

Producer: Christopher West

About this century performance *The Times* said: 'Covent Garden does well to muster such a cast from within its walls.' *Opera* commented on the fact that Dalberg's Ochs had been toned down considerably but that he and certain other aspects of the production lacked the feeling of aristocratic behaviour. A 'Surbiton tea-cloth' in Act I was mentioned. Barbara Howitt's Annina and McAlpine's Tenor were both much admired.

Royal Opera House, Covent Garden
1955/56 Season
October 29, 1955, for six performances in English

	October 29, November 1, 7, 1955	November 10, 16, December 5, 1955
Octavian	Shacklock	Shacklock
Marschallin	Fisher	Fisher
Baron Ochs	Dalberg	Glynne
Valzacchi	Nilsson	Nilsson
Annina	Howitt	Howitt
Tenor Singer	McAlpine	McAlpine
von Faninal	Ronald Lewis	Ronald Lewis
Sophie	Leigh	Leigh
Conductor	Kempe	Kempe

Designer: Robin Ironside

Producer: Christopher West

This was the last season in which these veterans of the opera, Sylvia Fisher and Constance Shacklock, sang their familiar roles together. Although Shacklock was to reappear as Octavian in 1959, the partnership was ending. Much of the opera's success over the past eight years must be attributed to these two artistes, and *The Times* praised them both warmly. 'Miss Sylvia Fisher's Princess which, besides being beautifully sung, shows countless new inflexions and subtleties of interpretation which few people would have suspected lay within her grasp when she first attempted the part'; and 'Miss Shacklock's Octavian retains all its youthful impetuosity and charm while maturing out of all recognition vocally.'

Dalberg's Ochs and Leigh's Sophie had both improved, and despite two mishaps on the stage (an overturned staircase in the Act II brawl, and Ochs's failure to remove his wig in Act III), *The Times* felt that the performance on October 29 'was one of those rare occasions when everything conspired towards perfection [during] three and a half hours of quintessential Straussian sensuous enchantment . . .'.

At the last three performances, Howell Glynne returned to give a finished performance as Ochs, and the rest of the cast, as before, was drawn from the resident Company.

Royal Opera House, Covent Garden

1958/59 Season
November 27, 1958, for six performances in English

	November 27, 29, December 1, 5, 1958	December 16, 19, 1958
Octavian	Töpper	Shacklock
Marschallin	C. Watson	Hale
Baron Ochs	Pease	Pease
Valzacchi	Nilsson	Nilsson
Annina	Howitt	Howitt
Tenor Singer	McAlpine	McAlpine
von Faninal	Ronald Lewis	Ronald Lewis
Sophie	Carlyle	Carlyle
Conductor	Kempe	Downes

Designer: Robin Ironside   Producer: Christopher West

A new cast of principals in a revival of the opera, after a pause of three years, brought a re-appraisal of *Rosenkavalier*. A German Octavian sang in (but knew no) English, an American Marschallin came from Frankfurt, an American Ochs from Hamburg, and an English Sophie, made her début with a 'splendid performance'. Andrew Porter in the *Financial Times* felt that the total effect was 'more Hofmannsthal than Strauss', and in the same newspaper he considered Töpper to be a 'moderate Octavian, below the Covent Garden standard set by Constance Shacklock at the last revival'. *The Times* remarked that 'she had the initial

103

advantage of looking like a handsome youth instead of a fat mezzo-soprano in boy's clothing'. In the *Sunday Times*, the charge was again laid of less Strauss than Hofmannsthal, and Kempe was blamed for achieving clarity and elegance at the expense of warmth and lilt.

Claire Watson (who had studied with Elisabeth Schumann and Otto Klemperer) was able to bring an aristocratic interpretation to the part of the Marschallin, which she sung 'with feeling and sincerity' (*Opera*).[1]

Opinions were divided over James Pease's interpretation, but it was well sung and consistently portrayed. *Opera*[2] thought he was 'outstanding . . . not for a moment did this Ochs forget his breeding and rank'.

Once more McAlpine was particularly mentioned and so was Barbara Howitt. The production was said to be accomplished.

Covent Garden Opera Provincial Tour, Spring 1959

New Theatre, Oxford
March 4, 1959, for two performances in English

	March 4, 1959	March 7, 1959
Octavian	Leigh	Leigh
Marschallin	Hale	Hale
Baron Ochs	Pease	Pease
Valzacchi	Bowman	Nilsson
Annina	Berry	Howitt
Tenor Singer	Kaart	Kaart
von Faninal	Allen	Ronald Lewis
Sophie	Carlyle	Carlyle
Conductor	Downes	Downes

Palace, Manchester
March 23, 1959, for two performances in English

	March 23, 1959	March 28, 1959
Octavian	Leigh	Leigh
Marschallin	Hale	Hale
Baron Ochs	Pease	Pease
Valzacchi	Nilsson	Nilsson
Annina	Berry	Berry
Tenor Singer	Macdonald	Macdonald
von Faninal	Ronald Lewis	Allen
Sophie	Carlyle	Carlyle
Conductor	Downes	Downes

Designer: Robin Ironside   Producer: Christopher West

[1] Vol. 10, No. 1, p. 61.
[2] Vol. 10, No. 1, p. 62.

Royal Opera House, Covent Garden
1958/59 Season
May 27, 29, June 3, 1959, for three performances in English

Octavian	Shacklock
Marschallin	Hale
Barno Ochs	Pease
Valzacchi	Nilsson
Annina	Howitt
Tenor Singer	Macdonald
von Faninal	Ronald Lewis
Sophie	Carlyle
Conductor	Kempe

Designer: Robin Ironside   Producer: Christopher West

These three not very distinguished performances were somewhat overshadowed by the Glyndebourne *Rosenkavalier*, certainly as far as the casts compared on paper. Musically, however, Kempe's magic was again in evidence and 'what ennobled the performance was the orchestral playing, upon which the voices could float and soar. Mr. Kempe is wary of Strauss's tight texture, holds it on a light rein, is scrupulous about internal balance, and above all makes it flow on all-embracing rhythm which is conceived from the first bar in the long terms of each whole act' (*The Times*).

Constance Shacklock returned to her part of Octavian in which she was utterly at ease 'gracefully yielding the palm to Una Hale in the first act'. Miss Hale was 'growing towards an excellent Marschallin' (*Daily Telegraph*), and while she needed to acquire more authority, she had 'discovered how to pour a stream of really beautiful tone into the mouth of Strauss's eloquent phrases' (*The Times*).

Pease was castigated for cheapening his performance and for including 'an American wolf-whistle' (*Daily Telegraph*). 'His voice does not come away from him with the freedom that its resonance leads one to expect' (*The Times*).

Joan Carlyle was vocally strong and 'an unusual spitfire of a Sophie well able to stand up to her father' (Ronald Lewis), 'a realistic sycophant' (*Daily Telegraph*).

Opera Magazine welcomed the news that this would be the last Covent Garden production of *Rosenkavalier* in English, describing it as 'keyed in a low comedy vein [lacking] elegance, breeding and charm'.

The Opera House, Glyndebourne
1959 Season
May 28, 30, June 3, 5, 7, 9, 16, 18, 20, 23, 26, 28, 30, 1959 for thirteen performances in
   German

Octavian	Söderström
Marschallin	Crespin

Baron Ochs	Czerwenka
Valzacchi	Kentish
Annina	N. Evans
Tenor Singer	McAlpine
von Faninal	Ferenz
Sophie	Rothenberger
Conductor	Ludwig

Designer: Oliver Messel   Producer: Carl Ebert

Those who attended the first performance found that their pink programme book (embellished with two silver roses) had a card, attached to the white tasseled cord threaded through it, which read:

Glyndebourne Festival Opera House
28th May 1959
The first public performance of Richard Strauss's *Der Rosenkavalier* at Glyndebourne, given before an audience of Members of the Glyndebourne Festival
Society to mark the Twenty-fifth Anniversary of the founding of Glyndebourne Opera and to pay tribute to the work of Professor Carl Ebert at
Glyndebourne

The Press was invited, but the notice in *The Times* on the following day led to an unfortunate incident. Mr. Christie remonstrated (in vain) with this newspaper, circulated letters to those who had paid to attend the performance and solicited their help in reversing *The Times* music critic's views.

The general criticisms were aimed at Glyndebourne's acoustics for this opera; the need to achieve the correct balance between orchestra and voices; the smallness of the auditorium which threw the audience upon the orchestra; and a lack of space on the stage. But these were easily over-shadowed in the rest of the Press by enormous praise of Carl Ebert's swan-song. It was a superb production in which 'loving and detailed rehearsal, preparation by a large and devoted music staff, and the sheer inspiration that comes from having such a director as Ebert in charge', all told (*Financial Times*). There were some wistful regrets that Fritz Busch had not been able to combine with Ebert in the realisation of the work at Glynde-bourne—a hope they had in the middle thirties[1].

Oliver Messel's 'rococo fantasy' (*Daily Telegraph*) 'conceived frankly and fully in the manner of Roller, [is] possibly the most beautiful he has ever designed' (*Financial Times*).

Régine Crespin (from Paris) was a Marschallin 'somewhat ample for the Glyndebourne stage, but of unimpeachable dignity and distinction. If she was rather more credible as the

---

[1] 'They even discussed the project with Strauss who, it seems, agreed to make a smaller orchestral version to match the dimensions of Mr. Christie's theatre. But Strauss delayed in producing his reduced version; the war came, and by the time its clouds had properly cleared once more, he was dead' (*Observer*).

great lady than as the smiling sensualist, that was probably due in part of her singing the role for the first time in a language foreign to her. . . . She was at her best in the last act' (*Sunday Times*).

'Miss Elizabeth Söderström (from Stockholm) was as perfectly ambisexual an Octavian as could ever be encountered and she sang with a fine strong voice that could take on all the inflexions and colours from calf-love to true love, and from anger to mockery' (*The Times*).

And as Sophie, Annelies Rothenberger (from Munich) was 'dramatically and visually ideal, neither doll nor spitfire . . .' (*Sunday Times*). 'Exquisitely sung' (*Observer*). 'No singer that I have ever heard in this part has suggested so well the pride rather than the timidity of innocence' (Martin Cooper: *Daily Telegraph*).

As Ochs, Oscar Czerwenka (who sang with a native Viennese accent) was perhaps too lusty. But he 'had the great merit of remaining lovable despite his grossness. His voice lacks the full range demanded by the role but its earthy and vigorous character was ideal. . . .'

Andrew Porter in *The Financial Times* summed up with these words, 'This *Rosenkavalier* comes closer than I have ever seen to being a living presentation of the work that one got to know and love from the score, the old records and the old designers. All its richness and diversity are here, its heart-searching beauties, the sweet excitement of young love, the poetry of resignation.'

Royal Opera House, Covent Garden
1959/60 Season
December 4, 1959, for five performances in German

	December 4, 7, 10, 1959	December 14, 1959	December 17, 1959
Octavian	Jurinač	Töpper	Töpper
Marschallin	Schwarzkopf	Schwarzkopf	Schwarzkopf
Baron Ochs	Boehme	Boehme	Boehme
Valzacchi	Nilsson	Nilsson	Nilsson
Annina	Sinclair	Sinclair	Sinclair
Tenor Singer	Macdonald	Macdonald	McAlpine
von Faninal	Ronald Lewis	Ronald Lewis	Ronald Lewis
Sophie	Steffek	Steffek	Steffek
Conductor	Solti	Solti	Solti

Designer: Robin Ironside   Producer: Hans Busch★

★ The son of Fritz Busch.

Desmond Shaw-Taylor in the *Sunday Times* considered that '. . . the current *Rosenkavalier* revival is quite a splendid affair, strongly cast and thoroughly rehearsed, with a new and effective producer in Hans Busch, and with Robin Ironside's pretty but formerly somewhat flimsy sets notably improved for that occasion. Above all it has in Georg Solti the best Strauss conductor I have heard since the death of Kleiber. . . .'

With a cast that was up to the international standard of pre-war summer performance, it was sung in German and with guest artists in the principal roles 'all in one sense or another making *débuts*' (*The Times*). Elizabeth Schwarzkopf had last been heard in this opera as Sophie in 1950; Sena Jurinač had never appeared in it in Britain before; and Hanny Steffek was altogether a newcomer. They were to varying degrees satisfactory, dramatically and vocally, and in addition their voices blended beautifully in the trio.

Mme. Schwarzkopf was noticed by the *Financial Times* as having 'an artificiality in her interpretation . . . that she seems almost a trivial woman, not substantial as great Marschallins should be . . .; Jurinač played and sang Octavian with an unaffected sincerity that was perfect at every point. Nothing seemed studied; every inflexion and gesture was ideal. Hanny Steffek's Sophie was purely voiced, and expertly characterised.'

'The Baron Ochs of Mr. Kurt Boehme . . . carried the comedy in fine voice on a firm line that never degenerated into farce' (*The Times*). To him must go much credit for a Viennese authenticity; 'he is probably the only one of our day who, without exaggeration, can realise the whole role fully and richly and sing it well' (*Financial Times*).

The smaller parts, especially Ronald Lewis's Faninal and Monica Sinclair's Annina (a new role for her) were seen to have benefited enormously from Hans Busch's sensitive direction, and Desmond Shaw-Taylor concluded his article by saying : 'Whether or not performances of the opera in English are to be resumed at a later date, the present cast is assured of a warm welcome whenever it can be reassembled.'

The Opera House, Glyndebourne
1960 Season
June 10, 1960, for thirteen performances in German

	June 10, 12, 16, 19, 22, 25, 28, 30, July 2, 1960	July 6, 8, 10, 12, 1960
Octavian	Sarfaty	Sarfaty
Marschallin	Crespin	C. Watson
Baron Ochs	Czerwenka	Czerwenka
Valzacchi	Kentish	Kentish
Annina	N. Evans	N. Evans
Tenor Singer	Macdonald	Macdonald
von Faninal	Ferenz	Ferenz
Sophie	Rothenberger	Rothenberger
Conductor	Ludwig	Ludwig

Designer: Oliver Messel

Production rehearsed by Richard Doubleday

This was substantially the same cast as at the 1959 performances, except for a new Octavian in Miss Regina Sarfaty (from New York), and the current Tenor Singer from London, Macdonald, *vice* McAlpine.

Sarfaty 'was most successfully cast. She was so completely inside the role that it was hard to believe it a first performance' (*Financial Times*). 'She was triumphant in conveying the occasional petulance, the youthful bewilderment, and the growing maturity of Octavian, and she had a beautiful mellow voice, rich yet steady throughout its considerable range' (*The Times*). Once more it was observed that 'the small' orchestra cannot possibly muster the warmth of string tone to melt and merge the drier wind' (*The Times*), yet the whole production is 'distinguished by clarity and truthfulness of presentation' (*Financial Times*).

For the last four performances Claire Watson 'presented a valid and credible interpretation of the role of the Marschallin, although she looked a good deal younger than Mme. Crespin. Miss Watson's singing was firmer and more assured than when she was heard in the same role at Covent Garden in November 1958 . . . and . . . she launched the trio most beautifully' (*Financial Times*).

'Leopold Ludwig has taken the measure of the theatre and come to terms with the orchestra,' said *The Times*, 'so that there were tender pianissimos and long drawn phrasing in those parts . . . where dramatist and composer touch fundamentals.'

Royal Opera House, Covent Garden
1960/61 Season
October 24, 1960, for four performances in German

	October 24, 27, November 9, 1960	November 1, 1960
Octavian	Töpper	Töpper
Marschallin	Crespin	Hale
Baron Ochs	Langdon	Langdon
Valzacchi	Bowman	Bowman
Annina	Sinclair	Sinclair
Tenor Singer	Macdonald	Macdonald
von Faninal	Ronald Lewis	Ronald Lewis
Sophie	Carlyle	Carlyle
Conductor	Downes	Downes

Designer: Robin Ironside   Producer: Alfred Jerger

Having acquired Mme. Crespin for three performances at the Opera House, the management obtained the 'veteran and experienced Straussian Alfred Jerger (a former Covent Garden Ochs[1] and Mandryka[2])' to rehearse the production in as faithful a manner as possible.

[1] 1924. *q.v.*
[2] *Arabella*, 1934. *q.v.*

The Times considered that 'Mme. Crespin's Marschallin in the spaciousness of Covent Garden . . . was superb, still perhaps a little maturer than the young and beautiful 32-year-old envisaged by the composer, but offering a new dignity and authority that enabled her to take complete possession of the performance . . .'.

Michael Langdon, who was singing his first Ochs, had studied the part with Jerger in Vienna, and showed ample signs of becoming a very good portrayer of the part.

Herta Töpper's Octavian was 'rather too assured and knowing a boy . . . but an excellent Mariandel'. 'Edward Downes . . . reveals and controls the splendours of the score with authority' (*Sunday Times*). 'In sum, a performance which showed the Covent Garden Company at strength' (*Financial Times*).

Covent Garden Opera Provincial Tour, Spring 1961

New Theatre, Oxford
March 21, 1961, for one performance in German

Hippodrome, Coventry
March 27, 1961, for one performance in German

Octavian	Elkins
Marschallin	Hale
Baron Ochs	Langdon
Valzacchi	Bowman
Annina	Berry
Tenor Singer	Macdonald
von Faninal	Ronald Lewis
Sophie	Carlyle
Conductor	Downes

Opera House, Manchester
April 3, 1961, for two performances in German

	April 3, 1961	*April 5, 1961*
Octavian	Leigh	Leigh
Marschallin	Hale	Hale
Baron Ochs	Langdon	Langdon
Valzacchi	Bowman	Bowman
Annina	Berry	Berry
Tenor Singer	Macdonald	Turp
von Faninal	Ronald Lewis	Ronald Lewis
Sophie	Carlyle	Carlyle
Conductor	Downes	Downes

Grand Theatre, Leeds
April 10, 1961, for one performance in German

Octavian	Leigh
Marschallin	Hale
Baron Ochs	Langdon
Valzacchi	Bowman
Annina	Berry
Tenor Singer	Turp
von Faninal	Ronald Lewis
Sophie	Carlyle
Conductor	Downes

Designer: Robin Ironside   Producer: Alfred Jerger

Royal Opera House, Covent Garden
1960/61 Season
April 18, 21, 1961, for two performances in German

Octavian	Leigh
Marschallin	Crespin
Baron Ochs	Langdon
Valzacchi	Bowman
Annina	Berry
Tenor Singer	Turp
von Faninal	Ronald Lewis
Sophie	Carlyle
Conductor	Downes

Designer: Robin Ironside   Producer: Alfred Jerger

'The Summer Opera Season opened at Covent Garden last night with the return of last autumn's restudied *Rosenkavalier*' almost sounds like the beginning of a between-wars notice. But since the only guest was Régine Crespin, giving her 'gracious portrayal of the Marschallin which remains the focal point', the 129th performance of *Rosenkavalier* at the Royal Opera House, sung by a mature and excellent resident cast shows how far the Company has come.'

Adèle Leigh's first Octavian in London 'makes too much the giddy spineless boy of Rofrano; we can believe in him but not take him seriously'. Otherwise (*The Times*), 'her voice has become much bigger and darker so that it is now ably contrasted with the rich but bright dramatic soprano of Mme. Crespin and the light, silvery tones of Miss Joan Carlyle's Sophie'.

'Mr. Michael Langdon's Ochs is even better than before. . .now he has found fuller, more resounding tones in which to sing the music . . . Alfred Jerger's staging has held well' (*Financial Times*).

Royal Opera House, Covent Garden
1962/63 Season
October 2, 1962, for four performances in German

	October 2, 5, 1962	October 8, 11, 1962
Octavian	Seefried	Elkins
Marschallin	C. Watson	C. Watson
Baron Ochs	Boehme	Boehme
Valzacchi	Bowman	Bowman
Annina	Sinclair	Sinclair
Tenor Singer	Macdonald	Macdonald
von Faninal	Ronald Lewis	Ronald Lewis
Sophie	Holt	Holt
Conductor	Varviso	Downes

Designer: Robin Ironside   Production rehearsed by John Copley

'Style was the quality most conspicuously absent', said the *Financial Times* of this revival, yet this very fault was forgiven and forgotten as soon as the third act trio started. As the Observer said: '*Hab mir's gelobt* was unfolded with glorious radiance, at a tempo slower than usual.' 'What had begun as no more than a respectable performance (and sometimes even a little less than that) left respectability behind for something much loftier' (*The Times*). The three protagonists of the trio were Claire Watson who 'from the third act entrance gained authority and expressiveness, even vocal bloom' (*The Times*); Irmgard Seefried, singing Octavian for the first time in London, 'thrilling when a firm vocal line was required . . . she looked the part to perfection' (*Financial Tmies*), and 'an eager, exuberant Octavian' (*Observer*); and Barbara Holt, 'singing Sophia for the first time anywhere. She will surely grow into the part; at present she is better at suggesting Sophie's anger than her unworldliness or tenderness' (*Financial Times*).

The other two acts scarcely came up to the culmination of the last one. 'Mr. Kurt Boehme, whose Ochs worked tirelessly and with a resource that had to be admired to steal every scene and every situation' (*The Times*). 'What a pity it is when a distinguished artist so grotesquely overplays his hand' (*Financial Times*).

Kenneth Macdonald was described by the *Sunday Times* as the 'ideal Tenor', and the conductor Silvio Varivso was hailed by the *Observer* as 'an outstandingly gifted young conductor. The Orchestra played as if they were inspired, achieving miracles of delicacy and refinement in a score that is too often made to sound rowdy and pot-bellied, and every singer on the stage took light and fire from Varviso's presence.'

112

Royal Opera House, Covent Garden
1962/3 Season
March 7, 1963, for five performances in German

	March 7, 11, 1963	March 14, 18, 20, 1963
Octavian	Meyer	Meyer
Marschallin	Crespin	Crespin
Baron Ochs	Langdon	Langdon
Valzacchi	Bowman	Bowman
Annina	Sinclair	Sinclair
Tenor Singer	Macdonald	Macdonald
von Faninal	Ronald Lewis	Ronald Lewis
Sophie	Holt	Carlyle
Conductor	Wallberg	Wallberg

Scenery by Robin Ironside   Production rehearsed by John Copley

'It is high time, one begins to think, that this whole production was renovated. Much of it is threadbare and urgently in need of a fresh approach', said the critic of the *Daily Telegraph*. The impression of a routine performance was heightened by some new 'business', such as Octavian fetching the medallion from inside the bed in Act I; and his being present to give the 'Mariandel' letter to Annina and watch her deliver it to the Baron at the end of Act II. For whereas these production points were new to Covent Garden, one felt that they were more part of Kerstin Meyer's interpretation than of a fresh mind being brought to bear on the whole work.

Mme. Crespin shared the honours of the evening with Kerstin Meyer. The former '. . . returning to her old role . . . was supremely authoritative and moving in the last act' (*The Times*). 'Her impersonation of the Marschallin must be considered one of the outstanding operatic characterisations of our day. She was her customary sophisticated and subtle self on this occasion, above all in her famous Act I monologue '(*Daily Telegraph*).

And of Kerstin Meyer, David Cairns in the *Financial Times* had much to say that was not only descriptive but psychologically revealing. 'The most striking thing is Kirsten Meyer's Octavian. It is sung with fervour and musical understanding. . . . This is a very young Octavian—almost painfully young at times—a pale, narrowed face with burning eyes, a body whose impulsiveness is sometimes awkward and sometimes beautiful, an adoring, touchy, proud, sensual and nervously sensitive spirit. The Marschallin's prophecy that sooner or later he will leave her is an actual physical blow to him.

'Later in the same scene, when the Marschallin muses aloud on the lonely day she is to spend, the shining ecstasy of the gaze with which this Octavian regards her is profoundly touching. When Octavian first declares his love for Sophie, Miss Meyer contrives, in a remarkable way, by the pose of her head and the intentness of her look, to convey both the piercing happiness and the ephemerality of the experience. It is an instance of intense pathos.

'In the last act, disguised as Mariandel, she even suggests a touch of adolescent excitement a pleasurable fear from the consciousness of being sexually pursued by the Baron. It is altogether a most interesting performance.'

The *Daily Telegraph* declared that 'the Sophie of Barbara Holt was a disappointment; thin and brittle in voice and shallow in characterisation'; and *The Times* added, 'In manner she found it extremely difficult to suggest the necessary shy charm and innocence. There were moments in the second act, indeed, when she seemed to find Ochs's conduct much more fascinating than repellent.'

The more than usually successful Baron Ochs, Michael Langdon, 'has now matured out of all recognition, and the characterisation is all the more persuasive for its avoidance of the vulgar and easy ways of winning laughs' (*The Times*).

The *Guardian* thought that '. . . the conductor, Heinz Wallberg, was principally to blame for the . . . charmless account of the whole opera' since he 'failed completely to draw from the Covent Garden orchestra the sort of delicate playing that Kleiber first taught them'.

At the last three performances, Joan Carlyle resumed her accomplished interpretation of Sophie. It was fortunate that the three soprano voices of Crespin, Meyer and Carlyle blended so perfectly that one heard, for once, the right vocal colour in ensembles.

Kenneth Macdonald gave an exemplary account of the Act I tenor aria and 'Monica Sinclair enlivened the end of Act II with her incomparable Annina' (*Guardian*).

Summary of Performances

London	156
Birmingham	9
Manchester	16
Sheffield	11
Leeds	4
Liverpool	8
Newcastle upon Tyne	1
Edinburgh	10
Glasgow	7
Halifax	5
Croydon	2
Cardiff	1
Oxford	3
Glyndebourne	26
Coventry	1
TOTAL	260

ARIADNE AUF NAXOS I

ARIADNE I

THE PURPOSE OF WRITING *ARIADNE* was to pay off a debt of gratitude which both Strauss and von Hofmannsthal felt they owed Max Reinhardt for coming to the rescue of *Rosenkavalier* when it needed a strong producer. Accordingly, von Hofmannsthal drafted a one-act opera based on the Greek legend of Ariadne who, deserted by Theseus on Naxos, longed only for Death to deliver her. Bacchus comes and in him she finds Love instead. The opera would follow a new version of Molière's *Bourgeois Gentilhomme*, and just to make the proceedings even more amusing, von Hofmannsthal had woven in a set of commedia dell'arte characters: the total effect of the opera is masterly. We have von Hofmannsthal's own conception of the metamorphosis of Ariadne: 'Change is the life of life; it is the real mystery of creating nature. He who wants to live must subdue himself, must change, must forget. The story of Ariadne is, in truth, metamorphosis, a wonder of all wonders, the secret of love. Ariadne loves and lives. She was dead and is resurrected.'

It is clear from this that von Hofmannsthal felt most deeply about his creation of this operatic Ariadne, for she is portrayed in his poetry elsewhere and we can sense a particular fondness for this work above his other creations with Strauss.

By introducing the calculated discord of the commedia dell'arte characters into the story, von Hofmannsthal was able to assist the metamorphosis by means of Zerbinetta (not originally in his plans as a character). Yet having seized on her, he describes her influence on Ariadne thus:

The problem is one of faithfulness personified in Ariadne, who can be only one man's wife or love or mourner. Her counterpart is Zerbinetta, who is in her element when dancing from one lover to another. Nothing short of a miracle, in fact a God, can redeem Ariadne. When she takes the God for Death she gives herself utterly to him as one would give oneself up to Death. What to Ariadne seems a miracle, appears to Zerbinetta as merely commonplace: the exchange of a new lover for an old one. So ironically the two worlds are made to meet in the end, though without the one comprehending the other.

Strauss composed some witty and pungent incidental music to Molière's Comedy, giving one now and again a whiff of what would follow in the opera.

But the difficulties of matching the demands of an acting cast of seventeen, an opera company of ten and thirty-six musicians in the pit are themselves as great as the problem of being able to please all the audience all the time. For those who come to see the play are not roused by the opera, and perhaps vice versa. So it is hardly surprising that there are only two productions to record, although the 1950 production was revived at Glyndebourne in 1962.

The Story of the Opera

M. Jourdain, a wealthy tradesmen, is determined to storm the barricades of exclusive society, and with that object in view he is initiated into the various polite accomplishments forming the equipment of a gentleman of fashion. The dancing master, the fencing master, the singing master, and even a professor of philosophy, are called in; and a tailor (rich in original and daring ideas) decks him in garments, which shame the plumage of parrot and of peacock. He also dips into logic, and makes sufficient progress in his education to discover that everything said or written is either verse or prose.

Madame Jourdain, a dear practical person, has no sympathy with her husband's ambition, even though he humbly offers to 'undergo a whipping before the whole world' if the chastisement will result in his acquiring the 'book learning' which is the heritage of every schoolboy. Nor does Madame Jourdain hold with her husband fawning on highly placed but parasitic persons who only batten on his weakness in order to relieve him of his money. M. Jourdain, having decided on a culminating effort, invites some of his titled friends to an amphitrionic repast, which is to be followed by an opera written round the legend of Ariadne's desertion by Theseus, and subsequent consolation at the lips of Bacchus. And lest some of the guests be bored by so serious an entertainment, a troupe of Italian buffoons is also engaged, the whole to be followed by a firework display aimed to take place at nine o'clock in the evening. In spite of an untimely interruption of the supper party by Madame Jourdain, who gives everyone present a piece of her mind in what her husband calls 'thoroughly middle-class style', this entertainment eventually takes place, but not quite in the manner originally intended. While the assembled company of singers and dancers are awaiting the signal to begin, a footman comes forward and announces a change in the programme. In order to save time and allow the fireworks to go off exactly at the appointed time, the opera and harlequinade, instead of being played the one after the other, shall be performed together. The composer of the opera and the singers are quite overcome by this amazing blow, but the dancers, who are not cursed with aesthetic scruples, can see no objection to the proposal, and finally persuade their colleagues to fall in with it.

M. Jourdain now appears with his guests, and the performance begins. The scene of the Opera is the island of Naxos, where Ariadne, deserted by Theseus, inhabits a lonely cave. Her three companions, Naiad, Dryad and Echo, are discussing her inconsolable grief, and lament her never ceasing longing for death. Ariadne next appears and delivers a long, heartbroken soliloquy which M. Jourdain finds exceedingly monotonous. Then Zerbinetta, Harlekin, Brighella, Truffaldin, and Scaramuccio, the five members of the troupe of Italian dancers, endeavour to enliven Ariadne by means of a little exhibition of their art, but without producing the slightest effect on the mourner. Then Zerbinetta tells her that she, too, has suffered many a time from the same complaint, but has invariably risen to the occasion by accepting the first consolation that has come to her aid, and advises her sad listener to do the same, but Ariadne (in their love-affairs women vary strangely!) will not listen to this well-meant advice and retires into her grotto. Zerbinetta's friends here suggest that she might be employing her time in a more amusing way than by endeavouring to console a woman who has long ago made up her mind to be eternally miserable. Then follows an animated scene in which each one of the four men vies with the other in an attempt to make a sentimental impression on the fancy of their volatile companion; the latter shows a decided partiality for Harlekin.

Naiad, Dryad and Echo now announce the miracle of Bacchus' arrival; and as his voice is heard Ariadne leaves the grotto and listens spell-bound. She at first believes that Bacchus is the messenger of death for whom she has prayed so long. However, she soon discovers her mistake, and enthralled by the beauty and youth of the god, throws herself into his arms. As the enamoured pair retire from the scene, Zerbinetta and the others sing mockingly after them and then dance away.

M. Jourdain, who has peacefully slept through the entire entertainment, now awakes but finds that his noble guests have departed. Left quite alone he soliloquizes on the advantages to be derived from associating with the upper classes, and pathetically envies the indescribable something which enables them to do everything, 'even if it is rude', with such a fine air.

(Synopsis from Programme of May 27, 1913, His Majesty's Theatre, London.)

His Majesty's Theatre, London
Special Production by the Beerbohm Tree Company
May 27, 1913 (British première) for eight performances
The Play in English, the Opera in German

	May 27, 1913	May 28, 1913	May 30, 1913	May 31, 1913
Naiad	Winternitz-Dorda	Winternitz-Dorda	Winternitz-Dorda	Winternitz-Dorda
Dryad	Hoffman-Onegin	Hoffman-Onegin	Hoffman-Onegin	Hoffman-Onegin
Echo	Hellensleben	Hellensleben	Hellensleben	Hellensleben
Ariadne	von der Osten	von der Osten	von der Osten	von der Osten
Harlekin	Armster	Armster	Armster	Armster
Zerbinetta	Bosetti	Francillo-Kaufmann	Francillo-Kaufmann	Bosetti
Bacchus	Marak	Marak	Marak	Marak
Conductor	Beecham	Beecham	Beecham	Beecham

	June 2, 1913	June 4, 1913	June 5, 1913	June 7, 1913
Naiad	Winternitz-Dorda	Winternitz-Dorda	Winternitz-Dorda	Winternitz-Dorda
Dryad	Hoffman-Onegin	Hoffman-Onegin	Hoffman-Onegin	Hoffman-Onegin
Echo	Hellensleben	Hellensleben	Hellensleben	Hellensleben
Ariadne	Drill-Orridge	Drill-Orridge	Drill-Orridge	Drill-Orridge
Harlekin	Armster	Armster	Armster	Armster
Zerbinette	Francillo-Kaufman	Bosetti	Francillo-Kaufman	Bosetti
Bacchus	Hutt	Hutt	Hutt	Hutt
Conductor	Beecham	Beecham	Beecham	Beecham

Costumes and Scenery supervised by Percy Maquoid, R.I.
The Play adapted by W. Somerset Maugham, and produced by Beerbohm Tree, who played M. Jourdain; the Opera produced by Emil Gerhauser and T. C. Fairbairn

Interest was great, and among subscribers to these special performances were several members of the Royal Family, five crowned heads of Europe, five Ambassadors, the Prime Minister and Mrs. Asquith, the Dukes of Marlborough and Westminster, and Mr. and Mrs. Bernard Shaw and M. Saint-Saëns. The Press gave the production a cautious notice.

Mr. Somerset Maugham was criticised for his too modern and racy translation of the Comedy—Sir Herbert Tree was accused of being vulgar in his performance—and he was compared most unfavourably with Coquelin, who had played the part in French in the very same theatre only five years before. Miss P. Neilson Terry 'looked adorable as Dorimène, but had little to do'.

The musical side to the entertainment was voted a success, however, and all critics acknowledged Mr. Beecham's skill with the orchestra. This was a chamber orchestra 'in which thirty-six players and thirty-nine instruments gave not only opportunities for novel combinations of sound, but for each instrument to be heard solo. Consequently the very finest players were chosen' (*Observer*). Special praise was given to the pianist, Mr. Vernon Warner, and the critics were most interested in and impressed by Zerbinetta's aria, which the *Pall Mall Gazette* referred to as 'The Higher Strauss' and quoted the cadenza in full.

The *Morning Post* marvelled at the fact that the opera had been performed in London within a mere seven months of its première in Stuttgart, and congratulated Mr. Beecham on his shrewdness in acquiring the British rights and of combining forces with Tree in staging the work. This paper, while admiring Mme. Bosetti's singing of the Zerbinetta aria doubted the artistic merits of it and failed to understand the reason for its place in the score.

The *Observer* produced eight musical quotations and, in common with other newspapers, likened the Zerbinetta aria to a Donizetti show-piece, put in for its own sake; but the *Observer* critic admired this aria more than his colleagues, and congratulated Mme. Bosetti most heartily upon her performance of it.

Very little note was made of the acting, none of the costumes, settings nor general appearance (except that the visual side was 'supervised by Percy Macquoid, R.I.'); and the few pictures which exist give a patchy idea of what the production looked like. In the opera, apart from the praise lavished on Mme. Bosetti as Zerbinetta, and to Carl Armster as Harlekin, Eva von der Osten and Marak were both liked in their final duet. The music critics, in the main, were puzzled—if not put out—by some of the orchestral effects which Strauss achieved through Beecham, in the unusual combination of the 'orchestra of soloists' including 'a novel kind of harmonium (purely inoffensive), and the now almost inevitable celesta' (*Morning Post*).

Theatre Royal, Drury Lane

One special performance of two excerpts from the Opera, as part of the Strauss Festival in the autumn of 1947
Sunday, October 12, 1947

Naiad	Gartside
Dryad	Furmedge

Echo	Field-Hyde
Ariadne	Cebotari
Bacchus	Friedrich
Conductor	Beecham

Designed by Oliver Messel   Staged by Sir Thomas Beecham

Sir Thomas Beecham revived the lament and an abridged finale, as the only work to be *staged* during the festival. In a sense this production—if such it can be called in its brevity—was a foretaste of what was to come in 1950.

The Composer was in the audience, and the *Ariadne* excerpts were recorded. It was hoped to issue them as a souvenir of the occasion, but unfortunately the tenor did not quite come up to expectations and the records were never released.

Naiad, Dryad and Echo; Ariadne and Bacchus were the only parts sung. After Ariadne's lament there was a cut to the announcement of the arrival of Bacchus, and thence to the end of the opera, omitting Zerbinetta altogether.

These fragments of *Ariadne* must have been a novelty for post-war London, and the opera was doubtless considered to be one of those rare works, as unlikely to be staged in full as *Intermezzo*, an entr'acte from which was played beforehand.

King's Theatre, Edinburgh
Edinburgh Festival 1950
August 21, (Scottish première) 23, 25, 29, 31, September 2, 4, 6, 8, 1950 for nine performances
Play in English, Opera in German

Naiad	Springer
Dryad	Thomas
Echo	Cantelo
Ariadne	Zadek
Harlekin	Craig
Zerbinetta	Hollweg
Bacchus	Anders
Conductor	Beecham

Designed by Oliver Messel
The play produced by Miles Malleson, the Opera by Sir Thomas Beecham

At the third Edinburgh Festival *Ariadne* was staged in settings by Messel, and framed in an apt translation of the Molière play by Miles Malleson, in which he played the part of Monsieur Jourdain. The whole work was an outstanding success. The playing of the Royal Philharmonic Orchestra under Beecham was superb—Beecham, the champion of the work thirty-seven years before in London. The Glyndebourne Programme Book for 1953 gives him retrospective credit for a personal triumph in 1950, since (as might be expected) he was one of the chief advocates of staging the rare and hybrid apple of von Hofmannsthal's eye. Beecham, it may be noted, preferred *Ariadne I* so much to *Ariadne II* that he never conducted the second version.

Some doubts were cast as to the dramatic qualities of the opera, while it is interesting to observe how musical taste has changed to condemn (in 1950) the final duet, so much liked in 1913. But it was clear that this Comedy-plus-Opera is a kind of musical phoenix, only expected to appear at infrequent intervals, but always exciting and worthwhile when it does so, *providing* that the standard of acting is as high as that of the singing and musical accompaniment. Beecham made a number of cuts of his own in the opera, and Zerbinetta's aria was sung very well indeed by Ilse Hollweg in the original key of E, but in a shortened version.

The Opera House, Glyndebourne
July 19, 1962, for eleven performances
Play in English, Opera in German

	July 19, 21, 25, 27, 29, August 2, 4, 1962	August 8, 12, 1962	August 16, 18, 1962
Naiad	McAusland	McAusland	McAusland
Dryad	Allister	Allister	Allister
Echo	Noble	Noble	Noble
Ariadne	Tarrés	Tarrés	Tarrés
Harlekin	Blankenburg	Blankenburg	Blankenburg
Zerbinetta	d'Angelo	Grist	Grist
Bacchus	Richard Lewis	Richard Lewis	McAlpine
Conductor	Varviso	Varviso	Varviso

When Sir Thomas Beecham's 'curving grace and thrusting wit' (*Financial Times*) so distinguished *Bourgeois-Ariadne* in 1950, and an excellent team of actors carried the play with consummate skill, *Ariadne II* was scarcely remembered nor considered. Now, twelve years later, without Beecham, and with thirty-six performances of the second version at easy memory-length in the last nine years, comparison was only to be expected.

The version of the play used was the same as in 1950; Miles Malleson again arranged, translated, produced and played 'Monsieur Jourdain with finesse and cunning. Here is a real —a Straussian—character' (*Financial Times*). But there were, unfortunately, 'some rather awful performances from the Old Vic troupe' (*Financial Times*). 'To assemble a company of actors for Molière's *Le Bourgeois Gentilhomme* and another of singers for *Ariadne* on the same stage is difficult and extravagant[1]; more seriously we have to switch over at half-time from a play with music to an opera, and the shift is awkward' (*Sunday Telegraph*).

The extravagance is 'as impossible as Glyndebourne itself, part of whose function should be to put on what cannot be done under normal opera-house conditions'.

[1] Twelve actors; eight dancers; ten singers.

There are many musical felicities in the incidental numbers written by Strauss, 'familiar in concert performance but much more effective in their dramatic context' (*The Times*).

Of the singers, Gianna d'Angelo came in for criticism of her soubrettish interpretation of Zerbinetta. She sung, though, with complete accuracy, and capably ran the vocal gauntlet of the great coloratura aria. Enrequita Tarrés, the new Ariadne, 'seemed not quite ready for the heroic style or cantabile splendours' of the role; and 'it was the more experienced members of the cast, Mr. Richard Lewis as Bacchus and Mr. Heinz Blankenburg as Harlekin, chief among them, who gave most pleasure and showed by what standards Glyndebourne's *Ariadne* must be judged' (*The Times*).

After expressing some surprise that this version was revived at all, the *Financial Times* summed up by saying 'Oliver Messel's décors still please, but the production has lost its former certainty of touch. Silvio Varviso's pacing of the score is well-judged, his reading is capable but essentially superficial, without strangeness, or poetry, or even the delicacy that the commedia dell'arte scenes call for.'

On August 8 a new Zerbinetta in the person of Reri Grist, a coloured coloratura from America, delighted audiences and critics. 'The voice was soft-grained . . . her coloratura was agile and musical. . . . She looked charming and moved like a dancer' (*Financial Times*). '. . . when Miss Reri Grist . . . took over the part of Zerbinetta, some prettily sparkling rockets went whizzing round the theatre . . .' (*The Times*). The only criticism she received was of some slight carelessness, but '. . . the enchanting glitter of her voice made up for a good deal' (*The Times*).

This newspaper also noted that Miss Tarrés was giving a more assured performance now; '. . . in the concluding love duet she sang several phrases that carried the ring of glory in them. Her voice, like Ariadne, is just beginning to find itself; there are signs of treasure trove there.'

For the last two performances there was a new Bacchus. William McAlpine had sung the part abroad and was as familiar with it as—the *Financial Times* was at pains to point out—we were familiar with his costume, '. . . . Oliver Messel's idea of Hofmannsthal's idea of the eighteenth century operatic idea of a god'. Reri Grist had even improved on her first performance 'singing the coloratura role of Zerbinetta as superbly as I have ever heard any role sung at Glyndebourne or anywhere else'. Praise indeed from Arthur Jacobs.

The Times, after complimenting Miss Grist by calling her the star of the performance, noticed the able support of 'the comic quartet, with Mr. Heinz Blankenburg as an outstanding Harlekin'.

Summary of Performances

London	.	.	.	8 (plus the 1947 excerpts)
Edinburgh	.	.	.	9
Glyndebourne	.	.	11
TOTAL	.	.	.	28 complete performances

ARIADNE AUF NAXOS II

ARIADNE AUF NAXOS II

VON HOFMANNSTHAL HAD ALWAYS BEEN CONVINCED, after having seen the first *Ariadne* in performance with the Comedy, that he and Strauss were wrong, and that the hybrid entertainment was a mistake. His fondness for the Opera led him to consider doing what once Strauss had thought and hinted at: to write a prologue to the Opera, making it independent of the comedy and of straight actors, and with the stage Composer of the opera the central figure in it.

About this character he says: 'I have rewritten the *Vorspiel*, the dressing-room scene, with great zest and vigour; the Composer now occupies the very centre of the scene; he is symbolically a figure half-tragic, half-comic; the whole antithesis of the action . . . is now firmly focused on him . . . there is even a hint of a little duet (Zerbinetta-Composer).'[1] Von Hofmannsthal urged Strauss to stop trying to 'patch-up' the casting and acting difficulties in *Ariadne I* and to turn to 'the only remedy [which] has been on my desk for the past week'.

Strauss must have hurt von Hofmannsthal's feelings considerably by his harsh reply: '. . . the Composer, for instance: to set him actually to music will be rather tedious. I ought to tell you that I have an innate antipathy to all artists treated in plays and novels and especially composers, poets and painters . . . this new version will always look to me like a torso.'[2]

And so the matter rested until late in 1915 when von Hofmannsthal again approached Strauss, who agreed to set the words of the *Vorspiel* to music. In spite of protracted argument as to how the opera in the new version should end, Strauss had the final word over the characterisation of the Composer.

It must be remembered that the First World War was in progress and good male singers, especially tenors, were hard to find. It was partly for this reason, and partly also his innate predilection for the female voice, which made Strauss tell the Poet on April 6, 1916, that he had given the part of the Composer to Mme. Lola Artot.[3] 'The Rosenkavalier is the only possible casting for the young Composer,' he said.[4]

Von Hofmannsthal was astonished and declared 'the idea of giving the part of the young Composer to a female performer goes altogether against the grain . . . to turn him into a

---

[1] *Correspondence*, p. 169.

[2] *Ibid.*, p. 171.

[3] Mme. Artot was a celebrated soprano in Berlin and had been the first Octavian there.

[4] *Correspondence*, pp. 241–2.

travesty of himself which inevitably smacks a little of operatta, this strikes me as, forgive my plain speaking, odious'.

However, because of the way the two artists had of working together, the *Vorspiel* turned out so well that von Hofmannsthal wrote to Strauss two years later: '*Ariadne* was wonderful. You have done nothing finer, and it is worth while making every effort to search for something new in style along the lines of the *Vorspiel*—and find it we shall.'[1]

Instead of Mme. Artot being cast as the Composer for the première of *Ariadne II* at the Court Theatre, Vienna, Strauss chose a completely unknown singer: Lotte Lehmann.

The changes in the opera itself are important. It now ends, appropriately, with the voice of Bacchus, and although Zerbinetta does re-enter, it is very briefly—hers is not the last singing voice to be heard. But her famous aria is still vocally the centrepiece, although simplified, shortened and transposed down a tone. Zerbinetta's long second aria, which announced the arrival of Bacchus is cut and thus the trio for the nymphs assumes far more urgency. By these means, too, Zerbinetta's part is crystallised more clearly.

The Prologue is in the nature of a conversation between the characters with few set-piece arias or duets. Musically this was a new form for Strauss, which he took to its culmination in his last opera *Capriccio* (*q.v.*). It is significant that M. Jourdain does not appear at all, but has his commands conveyed by his Major Domo—a speaking part. The role of the Composer, in the line of Cherubino and Octavian, is very rewarding to the soprano who sings it, and while both we and she could wish for a longer part, it is nevertheless a complete entity, embodying more in half an opera than many another, spread across three acts.

The Story of the Opera

Ariadne auf Naxos was produced at Stuttgart on October 24, 1912, and at that time was a musical perversion of Molière's *Le Bourgeois Gentilhomme*. Hugo von Hofmannsthal, the librettist, later prepared a fresh version of his story which Richard Strauss in his turn rearranged for music, and what was practically a new work was staged at the Vienna Opera on October 4, 1916.

The plot of this new version may thus be summarised: A pompous aristocrat, who by the way does not figure on the stage, has the idea of giving an entertainment at his house, and, posing as one interested in high art, engages a musician to compose a short opera for the occasion. But when he hears that the story is of a classic nature and that the action takes place on a desert island, he doubts whether this would please his guests. So he engages artists to follow up the opera with a bright harlequinade. At the last moment he realises that there would not be time to give the two performances consecutively, having arranged for a display of fireworks as a finale to the festivities, so he decides to have both entertainments done at the same time, much to the anguish of the composer and much to the delight of the Italian troupe who find ample scope to enliven the serious part.

The scene of the second section of the opera discloses Ariadne lying on a desert island where she has been abandoned by Theseus, and where she is found lamenting her fate until

[1] *Correspondence*, p. 398.

Bacchus arrives. In the meantime Zerbinetta is wooed by her associates Harlequin, Scara-mouche, Truffaldino and Brighella, but she light-heartedly indicates that if she marries at all, her choice will fall on Harlequin. The curtain falls with the union of Bacchus and Ariadne.

(*Argument from Programme of May 27, 1924, Royal Opera House, Covent Garden.*)

Royal Opera House, Covent Garden

May 27, 31, 1924 (British première of revised version) for two performances in German

Music Master	Renner
Composer	Schumann
Tenor (Bacchus)	Fischer-Niemann
Zerbinetta	Ivogün
Soprano (Ariadne)	Lehmann
Harlequin	Renner
Naiad	Jokl
Dryad	Jung
Echo	Landwehr
Conductor	Alwin

Designer not stated   The Stage under the direction of Charles Moor

Oddly enough, the first of these two performances took place exactly eleven years, to the day, after the first London performance of *Ariadne I*, but without the advance publicity, general interest or full house. In fact, this new version seemed to make little impression on the public, although Zerbinetta's aria claimed a good deal of space in the Press, as before.

The *Daily Telegraph* gave the longest and soundest appraisal of the production, with its scenery from Vienna; with Lotte Lehmann as Ariadne, making her first real impact on London; with Elizabeth Schumann as the Composer and her (real-life) husband Karl Alwin conducting; and with the Hungarian soprano Maria Ivogün as Zerbinetta. Ivogün's performance of the aria is fortunately preserved for us on a gramophone record, so that it is possible for us to understand why the *Daily Telegraph* said: '. . . she used her voice with an ease and a perfection of control, rhythmic and otherwise, that bespeaks the exceptional artist'.

The *Morning Post* professed to be bored with the whole thing up to Mme. Ivogün's aria, which was described as a brilliant achievement, while the critic of *The Times* only noticed Mme. Schumann and appears to have left after the Prologue.

So the opera was not voted a success, and the suggested reason for this, given twelve years later by Ernest Newman, was 'the fantasy of the two jumbled-up operas is apt to lose its point before a foreign audience unable to follow the subtleties of von Hofmannsthal's mind'. It is also unlikely that London opera-goers of 1924 were entirely prepared for von Hofmannsthal's 'very literary, very artistic and artificial' creation, divorced from the play which gave it its impetus.

Royal Opera House, Covent Garden
Visit of the Dresden State Opera
November 6, 1936, for one performance in German

Music Master	Schellenberg
Composer	Wieber
Naiad	Trötschel
Dryad	Jung
Echo	Wieber
Ariadne	Fuchs
Harlekin	Schellenberg
Zerbinetta	Sack
Bacchus	Ralf
Conductor	Strauss

Scenery: Adolf Mahnke   Producers: Hans Strobach and Josef Gielen
Costumes: Ernst Stern

This single performance of *Ariadne II*, under the hand of Richard Strauss himself, ensured that all places in the Opera House were taken well in advance. Since this was the only opera he conducted during the visit of the Dresden Company, it probably contributed more to a box office success than to the public's feelings about the work itself.

Ernest Newman praised the conductor and the score, but was less kind about the performance, chiefly because he could not accept the combination of the two sets of characters. He had particular praise for Arnold Schellenberg's Music Master and Harlekin, but described *Ariadne II* as 'the most interesting failure in the history of opera'.

As usual, the Zerbinetta rondo came in for more than a fair share of praise and space, but *The Times* thought that Erna Sack made the interpretation of it too obviously difficult. Marta Fuchs and Torsten Ralf, as Ariadne and Bacchus 'made the beauty of the mounting climax obliterate what had gone before'. About Richard Strauss, *The Times* said: 'What appealed most was the mellowness of most of the music and the ease with which in conducting it he obtained what he wanted from the singers and players without any physical effort on his part.'

W. J. Turner, in the *Illustrated London News*, declared he would 'almost go so far as to say that in some respects *Ariadne* is the finest of all [Strauss's] operas'. A bold statement, in view of the repeated successes—almost annually—of *der Rosenkavalier*, when contrasted with the infrequent productions of *Ariadne*.

The Opera House, Glyndebourne
June 24, 26, 28, July 1, 9, 11, 18, 24, 1953, for eight performances in German

Music Master	Bruscantini
Composer	Jurinač

Zerbinetta	Dobbs
Naiad	Graham
Dryad	Thomas
Echo	Cantelo
Ariadne	Dow
Harlekin	Gester
Bacchus	Richard Lewis
Conductor	Pritchard

Designer: Oliver Messel   Producer: Carl Ebert

This production, a re-appraisal by Carl Ebert of the 1950 *Ariadne*, may be said to have placed the second version of the opera well and truly in public favour. While Ernest Newman still preferred the *Bourgeoise-Ariadne* from personal motives, he was full of admiration for this production and said: 'Perhaps this is the most completely unified thing [Glyndebourne has] ever given us. Oliver Messel's settings, Carl Ebert's production, the singing and the playing under John Pritchard merge into a single whole.' He went on to congratulate the singers, particularly Sena Jurinač as the Composer and Mattiwilda Dobbs as Zerbinetta.

Because *Ariadne II* makes a short evening's entertainment, it was decided to preface the whole work with the full orchestral suite which Strauss put together in 1918 from the incidental music to the Comedy. It was too long and not quite well enough played to sustain thirty-five minutes or so in a semi-dark auditorium, with the curtain up, and the scene of the Prologue to gaze on. Artistically it seemed the perfect bridge between the two versions of *Ariadne*, but on reflection they must be thought of as two separate entities. There is little merit in an attempt to recall I before presenting II.

The casting of the work could scarcely be improved on. Sena Jurinač as the Composer gave a performance rich in understanding, full of emotion, and with singing of great quality. David Franklin's splendidly pompous Major Domo was a delight, and his German with a heavy English accent seemed intensely comical in the context of the Prologue. As Bacchus, Richard Lewis proved himself to be a leading tenor of enormous potential; and Bruscantini admirable as the Music Master. Last, but by no means least of the principal parts, Mattiwilda Dobbs excelled, both visually and audibly, as Zerbinetta.

Oliver Messel had slightly modified his 1950 setting for the Island, and now added a fitting scene for the Prologue.

The Opera House, Glyndebourne
June 25, 1954, for six performances in German

	June 25, 27, July 4, 7, 19, 1954	June 30, 1954
Music Master	G. Evans	G. Evans
Composer	Jurinač	Jurinač
Zerbinetta	Dobbs	Hollweg
Naiad	Springer	Springer

131

	June 25, 27, *July 4, 7, 19, 1954*	*June 30, 1954*
Dryad	Berry	Berry
Echo	Malbin	Malbin
Ariadne	Amara	Amara
Harlekin	Gester	Gester
Bacchus	Richard Lewis	Richard Lewis
Conductor	Pritchard	Pritchard

Designer: Oliver Messel   Producer: Carl Ebert

With three changes in cast, this production was otherwise similar to last year's. The chief difference was an improvement all round, an even greater enjoyment from the Opera, perhaps due to a better understanding of it.

The new Ariadne was sung in a most accomplished fashion by Lucine Amara of the Metropolitan Opera, New York, and the new Music Master was Geraint Evans. This very talented singer put age on his character and made him most endearing. Sena Jurinač was, if possible, more radiant than she had been in the previous summer, and Andrew Porter, writing of her performance in the *Financial Times*, said: 'No one who has seen it will ever forget Mme. Jurinač's Composer, a performance perfect on every level: sung, so older opera-goers say, as Lotte Lehmann sang, with radiant, soaring tone; adorably acted.' And comparing her singing in 1954 with that of 1953, *The Times* said: it was 'even more highly concentrated, more sheerly beautiful'; while the *Sunday Times* said: '. . . The triumph of the evening was Sena Jurinač's: her utterly captivating performance as the Composer would be hard to approach.'

The third change in cast was the inclusion of another American soprano, Elaine Malbin, as Echo. Miss Malbin also sang in the opera which formed the first part of the evening's entertainment, and about which the Press were concerned. This was Busoni's *Arlecchino*—an interesting choice at any time, but in this instance and on paper, a most intelligent one. *The Times* said: 'Both complicate to the point of obscurity their plots with a harlequinade; both intrude without rational justification a speaking part; both convey secondary meanings, the one satirical, the other psychological.' But there any comparisons end. Eric Blom in the *Observer* found that the Busoni work had no memorability but '*Ariadne* has this in abundance, ringing in one's head even after a first hearing and pursuing one in bath and bed. It simply wiped out *Arlecchino* there and then. . . .'

King's Theatre, Edinburgh

Glyndebourne Opera at the Seventh Edinburgh Festival

August 24, (Scottish première of second version) 26, 28, September 3, 8, 10, 1954, for six performances in German

Music Master	G. Evans
Composer	Jurinač
Zerbinetta	Dobbs

Naiad	Springer
Dryad	Berry
Echo	Malbin
Ariadne	Amara
Harlekin	Gester
Bacchus	Richard Lewis
Conductor	Pritchard

Designer: Oliver Messel   Producer: Carl Ebert

This was the 1954 Glyndebourne production transferred bodily to the North, and with the same cast except for James Atkins as the Major Domo. The production was, according to *The Times*, now running 'with a smoothness that permits every drop of its sweetness to be fully savoured'. Ernest Newman complimented Miss Amara on her singing, but considered that she appeared a trifle static.

Eric Blom, in the *Observer*, made an interesting observation when he pointed out that despite the instructions received from M. Jourdain that *die beiden Stücke, das lustige und das traurige, mit allen Personen und der richtigen Musik . . . gleichzeitig aus seiner Buhne serviert zu bekommen*, we hear only *der richtigen Musik* for the serious work, and not the music which the Commedia dell'Arte troupe must have used. Instead of dovetailing the two episodes, might they not have been set contrapuntally, Mr. Blom asks, thereby making an astounding *tour de force*. This undoubtedly occurred to Strauss, upon whom the brunt of the work would rest; and if the opera in its present form is still criticised for being too obscure, how much more so would it be if elaborated to this extreme.

The Opera House, Glyndebourne
July 5, 1957, for eight performances in German

	July 5, 7, 14, 20, 1957	July 12, 16, 24, 1957	July 18, 1957
Music Master	Hemsley	Hemsley	Hemsley
Composer	Söderström	Söderström	Söderström
Zerbinetta	Engele-Coertse	Barabas	Graham
Naiad	Schwaiger	Schwaiger	Schwaiger
Dryad	Sinclair	Sinclair	Sinclair
Echo	Lorengar	Lorengar	Lorengar
Ariadne	Amara	Amara	Amara
Harlekin	Blankenburg	Blankenburg	Blankenburg
Bacchus	Lloyd	Lloyd	Lloyd
Conductor	Pritchard	Pritchard	Pritchard

Designer: Oliver Messel   Producer: Carl Ebert

Lucine Amara turned out to be the only principal singer to carry forward the production of three years before, singing boldly and sensitively and with further insight into the character.

The new Composer was Elisabeth Söderström, who, faced with the unenviable task of following Sena Jurinač, did so with 'a different voice but equally great personal charm' (*The Times*). She managed to rise to the great occasion at the end of the Prologue, when music is glorified, and to make her own interpretation acceptable and magnetic.

Ill-health befell Miss Rita Streich, who was unable to sing the role of Zerbinetta as advertised. The part was shared by three singers during the season, none of whom was able to match the performance of Mattiwilda Dobbs in recent years.

The production was not as well-knit as before, and the comedians, particularly, were inclined to excite 'embarrassment more than mirth' according to *The Times*. Thomas Hemsley's 'ingenious, down-at-heel characterization' of the Music Master was particularly noticed, as was the wonderfully curious acting of the eccentric Hugues Cuenod as the Dancing Master. But *Ariadne* as a team in a production had gone off, as any performances do when there are understudies playing. For those who remembered it before, there was little to commend this revival, save Miss Söderström and, of course, the Ariadne herself.

The other opera in the programme (also an opera about opera) was Mozart's *Schauspieldirektor*.

The Opera House, Glyndebourne
July 17, 19, 21, 23, 25, 27, 29, 31, 1958, for eight performances in German

Music Master	G. Evans
Composer	Pilarczyk
Zerbinetta	Streich
Naiad	Delman
Dryad	Sinclair
Echo	Lorengar
Ariadne	Amara
Harlekin	Blankenburg
Bacchus	Richard Lewis
Conductor	Pritchard

Designer: Oliver Messel   Producer: Carl Ebert

This year, Ariadne was again sung by Lucine Amara, her Bacchus was Richard Lewis, returned once more after four years' absence, and a Zerbinetta postponed in Rita Streich. Vocally Miss Streich was well able to tackle the famous aria (as was anticipated from her interpretation in the Columbia recording of the opera) but her stage performance was disappointing.

The part of the Composer was taken by Helga Pilarczyk, better known for intensely dramatic rather than romantic roles. Neither her approach to the character nor her appearance —gaunt and slightly frightening—seemed suited to the ardent, impetuous and sentimental boy.

This year, *Ariadne*'s companion-piece was Wolf-Ferari's opera-buffa *Susanna's Secret*, sung in Italian. Yet for more than one spectator, *Ariadne* alone made a sufficiently full evening.

Sadler's Wells Theatre

1960/61 Season
January 25, 1961, for eight performances in English

	January 25, 1961	January 31, February 2, 4, 23, 1961	February 14, March 4, 7, 1961
Music Master	Turgeon	Turgeon	Turgeon
Composer	Jenkins	Jonič	Jonič
Zerbinetta	Bronhill	Bronhill	Bronhill
Naiad	Woodland	Woodland	Woodland
Dryad	Kells	Kells	Kells
Echo	Guy	Guy	Guy
Ariadne	Fretwell	Fretwell	Fretwell
Harlekin	Moyle	Moyle	Moyle
Bacchus	Remedios	Remedios	Craig
Conductor	Davis	Davis	Davis

Designer: Peter Rice   Producer: Anthony Besch

Not since 1939 had Sadler's Wells produced a Strauss opera, and the event proved to be a great success. After many seasons of the Ebert–Messel–Pritchard production at Glyndebourne, it was refreshing to see and hear the work in an entirely new style. Sung in English, clothed with less elegance, produced with less effect (and several blemishes) and performed in a theatre with notorious acoustics, the Sadler's Wells production must be regarded in an entirely different way from that of Glyndebourne, and there shall be no further comparisons.

To translate von Hofmannsthal into English is to lose straight away the depth of meaning in most of the Prologue and the mysticism which he put into his words throughout. But to an English audience, much more of the meaning on the lower levels got across and helped to create an early *rapprochement* between audience and singers.

Once one had settled oneself into accepting an English (and acutely unfamiliar) *Ariadne*, and not waiting for the well-known lines, it became easy to enjoy and also to appreciate what a very fine job the young Colin Davis was making of the score.

Unluckily, the Composer and the Bacchus had to be replaced on the first night because of an influenza epidemic, and there was more than a feeling of nerves on that occasion. But Gwynneth Jenkins and Alberto Remedios gave very adequate performances in the circumstances. Later on, when the cast had settled down, it was easier to get an impression of their true ability. Apart from the production of the Commedia dell'Arte troupe which, as *The Times* said, was 'nearer to the Crazy Gang than to Caillot or Gozzi', the total *effect* was right.

Elizabeth Fretwell was excellent as Ariadne, pouring out 'sumptuous, dignified phrases', and if Alberto Remedios as Bacchus had seemed more forthcoming, and less pondering on his experiences with Circe, the last scene, with its magic effect of the disappearing island would have added the touch of heart where it was most needed.

June Bronhill as Zerbinetta was able to execute the famous aria in exemplary style, but otherwise her singing was pinched and staccato, her acting too saucily modern.

135

Sadler's Wells Theatre

1961/62 Season

November 9, 15, 17, 21, 25, 1961, for five performances (four public, and one private on November 21 for 'Youth and Music') in English

Music Master	Turgeon
Composer	Morison
Zerbinetta	Studholme
Naiad	Woodland
Dryad	Cantelo
Echo	Guy
Ariadne	Fretwell
Harlekin	Moyle
Bacchus	Remedios
Conductor	Davis

Designer: Peter Rice

Producer: Anthony Besch

The principal changes in this revival were a new Composer—Elsie Morison—and a 'born Zerbinetta' in Marion Studholme, whose 'singing was a brave assault on the near impossible . . . but in the event the strain of coloratura took its occasional toll' (*The Times*). As far as characterisation went she was ideal.

Elsie Morison's 'pliantly phrased and deeply felt singing' showed the Composer's 'wistful idealism' (*The Times*). This was the first time she had undertaken the role and she made a complete success of it.

The remainder of the cast (except for the Dryad—April Cantelo, who had sung the part at Glyndebourne and Edinburgh) were as before and had gained in experience and assurance. Albert Remedios, the definitely cast though still wooden Bacchus, 'responded expansively to climaxes' (*The Times*) with Elizabeth Fretwell's Ariadne.

Philip Hope-Wallace in *Opera*[1] suggested that Sadler's Wells had made more of a success of their Strauss revival than had Covent Garden with *The Silent Woman*, 'because as a troupe the Company [at Sadler's Wells] had longer experience of putting over English'.

Colin Davis, recently promoted to Musical Director of the Wells, conducted ably but 'the only thing missing from the orchestra, which played admirably for him, was a certain gloss, the quality of best silk rather than of *crêpe-de-chine*' (*Opera*).[1]

Summary of Performances

London	16
Glyndebourne . .	30
Edinburgh . .	6
	—
TOTAL . . .	52

[1] Vol. XIII, No. 1, pp. 57-8.

136

ARABELLA

ARABELLA

WHILE FINISHING THE SCORING of *The Egyptian Helen* in June 1927, Strauss asked von Hofmannsthal to write 'a little one-act opera'—either gay or sad—a kind of curtain raiser for *Feuersnot*.[1]

On October 1, von Hofmannsthal described a scenario which he had drafted two years before, as 'a light opera (in the *Rosenkavalier* style, but lighter still, still more French if one can say that—still further removed from Wagner)'.[2] This was called provisionally *The Cabby as Count*, later *Arabella or the Cabby's Ball*, and swept away all Strauss's ideas of setting Turgenev's *Smoke*.

Strauss and von Hofmannsthal started work on the new project in December 1927, and on November 16, 1928, von Hofmannsthal ('practically') finished the second and third acts. Suggestions about modifying the first act were being requested by Strauss up to von Hofmannsthal's last letter to him, dated July 10, 1929, and accompanied by the final version of Act I. Five days later von Hofmannsthal died of a stroke. Strauss's telegram of congratulation on the finished work arrived too late for the Poet to read.

So ended the partnership of twenty-three years, and the influence of the Poet over the Composer; Strauss was to live and work for another nineteen years without his *alter ego*.

Arabella was performed in Dresden four years later, with the veteran soprano (and original Octavian) Eva von der Osten taking von Hofmannsthal's part as artistic director.

The Story of the Opera

'*Arabella*', described as 'a lyrical comedy in three acts', libretto by Hugo von Hofmannsthal (who has so frequently collaborated with Strauss, notably in *Der Rosenkavalier*), was produced at Dresden in July 1933. The scene is laid in Vienna in 1860.

ACT I

Count Waldner and his wife, Adelaide, live in a fashionable hotel, which they cannot afford. Owing to their extravagance and the Count's gambling they are ruined. The marriage of their daughter Arabella with some rich suitor will save them, and Adelaide is consulting a fortune-teller as to what prospect there is of this happening. According to the cards, a rich man will propose to Arabella, but someone will come between them.

[1] *Correspondence*, p. 431.
[2] *Ibid.*, p. 442.

Zdenka, Arabella's sister, is in love with a young officer, Matteo, and dresses as a boy, partly in order to be of service to Matteo in his hopeless passion for Arabella, who is quite indifferent to him, and partly because she is obsessed with self-sacrifice. She even writes Matteo love letters, pretending that they came from her sister. Count Elemer, another of Arabella's suitors, is anxious to take her to a ball. She consents, insisting that Zdenka, in her boy's clothes, shall accompany them. But the only man who has appealed to her is a tall Stranger she had seen in the street that morning.

Her father had meanwhile written to a rich friend, Mandryka, to borrow money, for matters are desperate, and the hotel will not even supply a glass of brandy on credit. A man calls on him. The Mandryka to whom he had written is dead: but this is his nephew who bears the same name and has inherited his immense wealth. The letter had contained a photograph of Arabella, and struck by its beauty, Mandryka now begs Count Waldner's permission to ask her hand in marriage. Waldner naturally consents, and is given bank-notes in plenty, with which he departs to gamble.

Arabella returns for a moment, nervous and depressed. "I feel as if someone were walking over my grave. . . . Is it the Stranger?"

ACT II

Mandryka is at the ball with Waldner, impatiently waiting to be presented to Arabella. When they meet he makes ardent love to her. She is a little frightened of him, but attracted irresistibly, for he is her mysterious Stranger. He mentions an old custom of the villages on his estate by which a girl who has promised herself in marriage hands a goblet of water to her man to mark the betrothal, "before God and man". Arabella accepts him but asks for an hour to dance with whom she pleases as a farewell to her girlhood.

Mandryka, wildly happy, consents, and orders champagne and flowers for everybody. But he discovers Zdenka giving Matteo an envelope which she declares contains the key of Arabella's bedroom, sent at Arabella's request. Zdenka, still humbly adoring Matteo, had been terrified by his threat of suicide owing to Arabella's coldness into this fantastic scheme. Mandryka is mad with jealousy, which is not lessened by a somewhat abrupt note from Arabella saying that she has gone home and will see him tomorrow. He is convinced that Matteo is her lover, and seeks to drown his agony in champagne, surrounded by a noisy crowd of guests.

ACT III

The lounge of the Waldner's hotel. Matteo finds Arabella alone, and with Zdenka's message to encourage him, rushes to her eagerly. He cannot understand her when she repulses him, thinks she is playing a part, and then accuses her of utter heartlessness.

Mandryka, arriving with her father and mother, announces that he is leaving Vienna by the next train. Waldner tries to make light of the incident, but Mandryka will not be pacified even by Arabella's protestations and by her appeal to Matteo to tell the truth and not to compromise her before the world and spoil her marriage just out of spite. Tragedy is looming near when Zdenka, no longer dressed as a boy, confesses her intrigue and the pathetic reason for it, praying through her tears for forgiveness. She wishes to take the blame, and on her knees begs them all to understand. Arabella forgives her, and Matteo, recognising her devotion and the strength of her love, realises that they can make each other very happy.

Mandryka's jealousy has vanished. Yet he is still puzzled and anxious, for Arabella has gone up to her room without even bidding him goodnight. When she asks him for some water, he thinks, forgetting the old village custom, she has done so merely to get rid of him. She reappears, and coming downstairs with the glass of water, hands it to him. The truth flashes on him. He drinks, smashes the glass to the ground, and embraces his betrothed.

(Synopsis from Programme of First Performance in London: May 17, 1934, Royal Opera House, Covent Garden.)

The announcement for *Arabella* in *The Times* of May 17, 1934, reads:

ARABELLA   Tonight at 8
(First performance in England)
Act I   Act II   Act III
8 to 9   9.25 to 10.7   10.20 to 11.10
Also to be performed on May 21st and 25th

A fourth performance of *Arabella* was put on specially in honour of Strauss's seventieth birthday on May 29.[1]

Royal Opera House, Covent Garden

May 17, 21, 25, 29, 1934, for four performances in German

Graf Waldner	Sterneck
Adelaide	Berglund
Arabella	Ursuleac
Zdenka	Borkor
Mandryka	Jerger
Matteo	Kremer
Graf Elemer	Bartolitius
Fiakermilli	Illiard
Conductor	Krauss

Costumes and Scenery by Benno von Arent   Producer: Dr. Otto Erhardt

Perhaps one of the reasons why *Arabella* was not well received at its first production in London was because the audiences were expecting 'another *Rosenkavalier*'. Mr. Ernest Newman's complaint to this effect was nevertheless anticipated by Richard Capell, in the

[1] The day after Glyndebourne had opened its doors for the first time with a performance of *Le Nozze di Figaro*.

Daily Telegraph, who had previously heard the opera in Dresden, and who felt the attitude of the comparison to be unreasonable. He added that 'an artist does not produce "another" of the thing he was doing twenty-five years ago . . .'.

The *Daily Telegraph* found the opera to be 'in point of taste and craftsmanship a master-piece' and said it was given in a highly accomplished way by a cast largely drawn from the Dresden première. Full praise was given to the conductor, Clemens Krauss.

The Times, while expressing some disappointment at the fact that *Arabella* was not another *Rosenkavalier*, nevertheless felt that the advantage was to be gained from the evidence that von Hofmannsthal was always setting Strauss new problems to solve, 'and therefore offering him fresh fields to conquer . . .'.

While the scene, in a residential hotel, may not be as pleasing as a Princess's boudoir, 'what is lost in external splendour is made up for by the more subtle drawing of human character'.

Ursuleac, Borkor and Jerger as 'a Tennysonian' Arabella; 'the pathetic boy-girl Zdenka'; and 'the hearty young Transylvanian bear-hunter Mandryka' respectively, came in for high praise, and the mid-Victorian settings and costumes were thought to be excellent.

The Times, in one of its direct summings up said, 'The first impression of the opera as a whole is that the composer repeats in it a manner to which he has long been accustomed and does so with only partial success.'

Royal Opera House, Covent Garden
Visit of Bavarian State Opera
September 15, 1953 for five performances in German

	September 15, 1953	September 17, 1953	September 18, 1953	September 21, 1953	September 26, 1953
Graf Waldner	Kusche	Proebstl	Proebstl	Proebstl	Kusche
Adelaide	Malaniuk	Malaniuk	Malaniuk	Malaniuk	Malaniuk
Arabella	Della Casa	Della Casa	Della Casa	Della Casa	Cunitz
Zdenka	Sommerschuh	Sommerschuh	Hermann	Trötschel	Trötschel
Mandryka	Uhde	Uhde	Born	Uhde	Uhde
Matteo	Fehenberger	Fehenberger	Fehenberger	Fehenberger	Fehenberger
Graf Elemer	Klarwein	Klarwein	Klarwein	Klarwein	Klarwein
Fiakermilli	Köth	Köth	Köth	Nentwig	Köth
Conductor	Kempe	Kempe	Kempe	Kempe	Reinshagen

Scenery: Helmut Jürgens   Producer: Rudolf Hartmann
Costumes: Rosemarie Jakameit

At the visit of the Dresden State Opera in 1936 the public was told that there was nothing to match the ensemble and cohesion of the *Company*. So did the Press again reflect on the advantages to be gained from a resident Company and orchestra working together over a long period.

The Bavarian State Opera was praised for its 'unity in production, a corporate individuality . . . a homogeneity and distinction of sheer, tonal quality . . .' (*The Times*).

The same critic, while tending to agree with the opinions of 1934 that Strauss had 'written himself out', nevertheless felt that there was much pleasure to be gained from 'the opulence, the sweetness, the sentiment, the vocal writing and the orchestral sonority, all the more that in these latter years all of these things are not only unfashionable but beyond our reach'.

Ernest Newman confessed to misjudging the work in 1934, perhaps because the performance then had not been as good as in 1953, but more likely because the audience were listening to the new work in the wrong way—with *Rosenkavalier* in mind all the time.

The *Daily Telegraph* upheld its former criticisms of the opera while praising the singers—as was general.

The two most significant performers were Lisa Della Casa as Arabella and Rudolf Kempe, the conductor. They were both making their débuts at Covent Garden. Mr. Kempe was praised for his feather-light handling of the score and the deft way in which he brought out the felicities, while avoiding over-emphasis and turgidity. Mr. Kempe was a 'find' and later became a familiar figure and a welcome one on the rostrum at the Opera House.

There was an extra performance of *Arabella* over and above those planned (just as there had been in 1934, but for a different reason). The first London performance of *Capriccio* had to be postponed from its advertised première on September 17, and *Arabella* took its place.

Although the Bavarian State Opera's season in London was not played to full houses by any means, *Arabella* was the best patronised of their three operas, and *The Times* wound up the season with a further notice of the changed cast on September 26, the last night.

Maud Cunitz as Arabella was said to have 'played it more vivaciously than Miss Della Casa, but she has not the sure vocal line and even production to get the best out of the final scene on the staircase'. Elfride Trötschel was thought to be an improvement as Zdenka, but the conductor could not match Kempe's handling of orchestra and singers.

Jurgens's sets were admirable, and the lighting in the final scene was an object lesson in artistic and artisan teamwork. Attention to detail and affection for the work showed in every aspect of Rudolf Hartmann's faithful production.

Summary of Performances

London   .   .   .   TOTAL 9

DIE LIEBE DER DANAE

DIE LIEBE DER DANAE

THE OPERA IS DESCRIBED as a mythological comedy, and the plot is known originally to have sprung from 'the tortuous fantasy of von Hofmannsthal' (as *The Times* put it). The sketch, which von Hofmannsthal left, was taken up by Strauss's latter-day librettist, Joseph Gregor, who tended to complicate rather than to give it intellectual depth.

The atmosphere of *Danae* certainly smacks of von Hofmannsthal with his love of obscurity, Greek mythology and parallel allusions to the present. But the plot is compounded of two unconnected legends; 'that of Midas whose touch changed everything into gold; and that of Danae, wooed by Zeus who, for this purpose, took the shape of a shower of golden rain' (*Radio Times*). Gregor's erudition seems, however, to have got 'the better of him at times, making him devote more space than is dramatically wise to irrelevant details of Greek mythology'.

The opera—under the title of *Midas*—was announced for performance in Vienna in 1939; the score was not completed until June 1940; and the première was rearranged to be the main attraction at Salzburg's 1944 *Theater- und Musiksommer*. It was intended to open the Festival with *Danae* on August 5, but only a special Dress Rehearsal took place on August 16. Viorica Ursuleac was Danae, Clemens Krauss conducted and Strauss was present. But because of Germany's worsening situation and the need for total war effort throughout the Third Reich, the Salzburg and all other festivals were cancelled and no public performance of *Danae* took place.

Danae was not publicly heard until its official première eight years later at the Salzburg Festival of 1952. Strauss's last opera *Capriccio* had already been performed in 1942, which will explain the apparently reversed opus numbers of his last two stage works.

The Story of the Opera

Jupiter, the Lord of the gods, came down to earth from time to time in search of amorous conquest. The jealousy of his consort, Juno, forced him to take sundry disguises when he wished to make love: thus to Semele he appeared as a cloud, to Europa as a bull, to Alcmene in the likeness of her husband Amphytrion, to Leda as a swan.

His latest prey is a difficult one. Danae, daughter of the King of Eos, Pollux, is both indifferent to the male sex, and passionately hungry for the glitter of gold, a passion hard to requite in bankrupt Eos. Jupiter appeared to her as a shower of gold but success did not blind him to the realisation that Danae was more interested in the precious metal than in the masculine force that propelled it. He therefore adopted another ruse. He endowed a penniless donkey-man, Midas, with the gift of transmuting whatever he touched to gold, and set this protégé on the throne of Lydia. In return for this, Midas was to change places with Jupiter whenever the god so wished; thus Jupiter hoped to touch Danae's frigid heart.

ACT I

Scene I: The Throne Room of King Pollux's Palace at Eos.

King Pollux is pestered by creditors whom he cannot pay, for he has already disposed of all the treasures in his palace, except for the royal throne. On their latest visit he attempts to appease them with the news that his four nephews and their wives have been sent to Lydia bringing Danae's portrait to the renowned and fabulously wealthy King Midas. Pollux hopes that Midas will fall in love with the portrait and, as son-in-law, help the kingdom out of its financial crisis. The sceptical creditors put little faith in this tale, and as a gesture strip the gold from the throne, seize Pollux's crown and depart.

Scene II: Danae's Bedroom.

An orchestral interlude describes the golden rain which now penetrates Danae's sleep for the second time. She awakes and recalls ecstatic memories of her shimmering visitant to her servant Xanthe, who sees little point in loving a phantom and regrets that Danae will welcome no rich suitor and so end all their troubles. At this moment Midas appears richly dressed, announcing himself as Midas's herald, the gold bearer Chrysopher. With a wave of the hand he turns the walls of the palace to gold and summons attendants who attire Danae in the same material. Danae is strongly minded to take Chrysopher, and ignore Midas, but the herald, although himself infatuated with her, is bound to conduct her to his master.

Scene III: A Hall in the Palace looking on to the sea.

The court, the creditors and the townsfolk have gathered to await the return of the messengers to Lydia. This royal octet report that Midas has fallen in love with the picture and is now on his way to Eos; they bring, as his love-offering, the branch of a tree which he has turned to gold. The wives of the four kings, however, have recognised Jupiter behind the mask of Midas; for they are no other than Semele, Europa, Alcmene and Leda, each of whom bears vivid recollections of past affairs with the god, which she hopes will be repeated on the present trip.

The creditors are prevented from seizing the branch, and with it Danae who is enchanted with her present, by the arrival of the golden ship in the harbour; muttering that such a costly ship will have to pay heavy harbour dues, they hurry to meet it. Jupiter, disguised as Midas, steps from the ship and greets first Eos, then Danae. He notes, too, that Chrysopher is betraying an excessive interest in Danae, who recognising the lover of her dreams, swoons to the ground.

ACT II

A Room in the Palace.

Semele, Europa, Alcmene and Leda are preparing the bridal chamber for Danae and her rich spouse, Midas. He, in the person of Jupiter, appears and is surprised to find himself recognised by the lively ladies. He confides in them the ruse to which he is forced by the jealousy of Juno, who had turned his last paramour, Callisto, into a bear. Faintly jealous of Danae, but still optimistic where Jupiter's attentions are concerned, the four queens retire, as Midas in his own shape appears. Jupiter warns Midas of his suspicions and reminds him, should he feel tempted to make advances to Danae, that whatever he touches turns to lifeless gold; it is, of course, Jupiter's intention to take Midas's place as soon as Danae is won over.

Midas is left alone as Danae enters the bridal chamber, escorted by a train of Cupids, and by the four queens who turn to the supposed Jupiter with honeyed words and, recognising the real Midas, run away. In a long duet, 'Niemand rief mich,' their attraction for each other grows ever more unrestrainable. Midas, begged for a sign of his power, turns the whole room into gold then, forgetting Jupiter's warning, folds Danae in his arms. She at once turns into a golden statue. Midas curses Jupiter and his fatal gift. The god appears and turning to the statue bids Danae choose the lifetime of gold that he can offer her, or Midas and penury. Danae's voice answers from the distance 'Midas . . . beloved'. Jupiter restores her to life, banishes the lovers to penury and, pouring scorn on her in an angry monologue, destroys the palace and vanishes.

ACT III

Scene I: An Oriental Highway.

Danae and Midas, now restored to his former humble position, are resting under a clump of palms. She is surprised to find herself impoverished. Midas explains what has occurred and, united in their love, they continue their journey singing a duet 'So führ' ich dich mit sanfter Hand'.

Scene II: A Mountain Forest in the South.

Angry and disappointed, Jupiter has sent for Mercury to bring news of Olympus whither he intends to return. Mercury relates the uproar of mirth with which the news of Jupiter's amorous failure has been greeted by the gods; even Juno laughed till she cried. They are on the point of setting off when the four queens arrive; Mercury has revealed the hiding place of their old paramour. The ladies mock Jupiter in a round-quartet 'Wie sehr er scherzt', and they all sit down to a picnic during which Jupiter bids a last farewell to the queens (he has already remarked rather ungallantly that they are all losing their charms in middle age). The sky turns dark, and the gods are once more preparing to depart when Pollux, his four nephews and the importunate creditors hurry in. They are chasing Midas, the king for his palace, the nephews for their abducted wives, the creditors because they cannot bear to see money elude them. At Mercury's suggestion, Jupiter disperses his pursuers with a handful of coins and a light shower of gold. He is still sad to leave the earth without seeing Danae again; Mercury advises him to seek her in the donkey-man's hut.

Scene III: Inside the Donkey-Man's Hut.

Danae, alone in the hut, sings of her love and her happiness even in squalid circumstances. An old man, wrapped in a burnous, enters the hut; it is Jupiter in the attire he wore on his first encounter with Midas. Jupiter comments on Danae's poverty and reminds her of the allure that she knew in her golden dreams. He relates the story of Maia (*Maja liebte er einst*) who lay in Jupiter's arms and vanished in the flowers that sprang up as nature's recognition of their love. Danae replies to this last temptation that her life, too, has been transfigured by love for Midas; Jupiter's attempts to regain her are vanquished by her love. She takes from her hair the golden jewel which alone remains to her of the gold that was Jupiter's gift; she returns it to the god as thankoffering for Midas. Profoundly moved by her devotion Jupiter realises that she has shown him the way to lasting happiness, gives his blessing to their union, and departs wiser and more contented. The theme of the duet *So fuhr' ich dich* tells Danae that Midas is returning home; joyfully crying his name, she runs from the hut to greet him, as the curtain falls.

WILLIAM MANN

Royal Opera House, Covent Garden
Visit of Bavarian State Opera
September 16, 1953 (British première) for four performances in German

	September 16, 1953	September 19, 1953	September 23, 1953	September 25, 1953
Pollux	Seider	Seider	Seider	Ostertag
Danae	Kupper	Rysanek	Kupper	Rysanek
Xanthe	Nentwig	Nentwig	Nentwig	Nentwig
Semele	Sommerschuh	Sommerschuh	Sommerschuh	Sommerschuh
Europa	Lindermeier	Lindermeier	Lindermeier	Lindermeier
Alkmene	Benningsen	Benningsen	Benningsen	Benningsen
Leda	Barth	Barth	Barth	Barth
Midas	Vandenburg	Vandenburg	Vandenburg	Vandenburg
Jupiter	Frantz	Frantz	Frantz	Bröcheler
Mercury	Klarwein	Klarwein	Klarwein	Klarwein
Conductor	Kempe	Eichorn	Eichorn	Eichorn

Scenery: Helmut Jürgens   Producer: Rudolf Hartmann
Costumes: Rosemarie Jakameit

The critics were sharply divided between condemnation of *Danae* and selection of its better aspects so as to praise it. The expensive production was a feast to behold. The effective translation of Midas's palace to gold was indeed magically done by ultra-violet light, especially as this was accompanied by one of Strauss's typically lush orchestral passages. The five orchestral interludes during the opera were excellently played by Kempe and the Bavarian Orchestra on the first night, Kempe once more displaying his characteristic deftness of touch with the score. Yet these interludes emphasised the trend towards symphonic music which Strauss seemed to find indispensable to underline the psychological goings-on upon the stage, and the work seemed long by the time the last act had even started. One critic voiced the phrase 'Strauss in decline' (*Observer*). But it is a rare opera and the opportunity of hearing it in performance was rightly acknowledged.

As Danae at the first and third performance, Annelies Kupper brought something of the authority of the creator, but Leonie Rysanek proved to be the better, all-round interpreter on the second and fourth nights. As Jupiter, Ferdinand Frantz (known hitherto in London only in *The Ring*) 'looked like Julius Caesar and behaved and fared like Wotan; he had most to do in sustaining the dramatic motion of the opera'. Howard Vandenburg as Midas and August Seider as 'a dignified bankrupt King' gave good performances (*The Times*).

After the first performance, Kempe left, and the orchestra was in the hands of Kurt Eichorn, a far less capable conductor. Another hearing under Kempe might have done much to help the listener. Smaller parts throughout were well taken, considering the fact that it was an opera in repertory.

The mixture of conventions tended to be overworked. If Strauss did gravitate towards Offenbach, it is debatable whether it was justifiable to dress the 'four mortal loves . . . in modern clothes as for the Côte d'Or'. This production pun may, by implication, heap another oblique allusion onto the pile already created by Gregor.

Summary of Performances

London .   .   .   . TOTAL 4

CAPRICCIO

CAPRICCIO

A conversation piece for music in one act

A GOOD DEAL OF OBSCURITY, if not mystery, surrounds the circumstances wherein this opera was first conceived and later born.

In 1953 Ernest Newman, then leading music critic of the *Sunday Times*, told us that *Capriccio* 'began with Strauss, after a practical experience as composer and conductor of operas such as no other musician has had since Wagner, finding himself putting in some hard thinking in 1940 about the nature and structure of that strange genre, which are today, after three centuries and a half, a greater mystery than ever to every thoughtful student of opera'.

The initial point of discussion with the conductor Clemens Krauss was the ancient one of whether the music or the word is basically the more important in any combination of the two. 'Gradually the discussion slipped almost imperceptibly from the plane of the abstract to that of the concrete, the stage figure of a Poet and a Composer beginning to define themselves. . . .'

This is contradicted by Joseph Gregor in the published correspondence between Strauss and himself. In a letter[1] which he wrote to Strauss from Vienna on March 27, 1939, Gregor says: 'I shall be bringing you the Casti work and my new version of the piece. The sketch which I made in 1935 is now no longer familiar to me.'[2]

The work referred to is a libretto by the eighteenth-century Italian Abbé Giovanni Battista Casti (sometimes called Gianbattista Casti), which was set to music by the popular composer of the times, Salieri, and first performed at Schoenbrün, Vienna, in 1786. The Salieri–Casti opera is called *Prima la Musica e poi le Parole* (First the Music and then the Words).[3]

But everywhere in the Strauss–Gregor Correspondence—and elsewhere in Strauss's case—the source-libretto is referred to as *Erst die Worte dann die Musik*, that is to say *Prima le Parole, doppo la Musica*, or quite often just *Parole-Musica*.

The straightforward reversal of the title by accident or design only complicates itself in the context of the completed Strauss opera. Also, the sub-title of *Capriccio* being what it is, gives no clue to whether the whole construction is an elaborate joke.

---

[1] *Strauss-Gregor Briefwechsel*, 1934–1939.

[2] Author's translation.

[3] The first person to suggest this subject to Strauss was, in fact, Stefan Zweig, in 1934.

Casti wrote no other libretto, neither is there a *Parole-Musica* libretto by anybody except Clemens Krauss; nor did Gregor's name ever appear on the finished work, which is credited jointly to Krauss and Strauss.

The opera *Capriccio* ('and what a wonderfully good-natured, humane and graceful work it is' —*Observer*) is an 'aesthetic discussion' with the added interest of Strauss's particular form of musically supported *conversation*, as opposed to *recitativo* or *parlando*, reaching its culmination. This treatment began with the Jews' argument in *Salome*, re-emerged at Baron Ochs's first entrance in Act I of *Rosenkavalier*, and almost found a new expression throughout the Prologue of *Ariadne II*. The process then took a different turn and stopped there in *The Silent Woman*, and reached full fruition in *Capriccio*, which Strauss called the codicil to his operatic Testament.

But while he may seem to have given full rein with words to his opposite number, the poet, Strauss kept his tongue in his cheek as Neville Cardus in the *Manchester Guardian* observed: '. . . So obviously is the old man [Strauss] enjoying himself in *Capriccio* that none but the solemnest Beckmesser would regard academically the issue supposedly in the balance of the libretto's argument. . . . But Strauss relishes playing the part of his own advocate, so much so that we can only feel sorry for anybody who lacks the humour, imagination and sense of irony and fun fully to enjoy this game Strauss is revelling in, with all the aces up his sleeve and knowing all the hands. . . .'

The opera is in one act and plays for two and a quarter hours. Even its professed opponents are silent about the last scene when 'the sound matches in magnificence anything Strauss has done before . . . here is live musical matter and true spontaneous feeling . . .' (*Opera*).

Throughout his compositions, Strauss had leaned towards the key of D♭ major when he wished to express a mood of particular beauty or remoteness. The tenor song and final trio in *Rosenkavalier*, the finale of *Ariadne* are three among many more. As he laid down his operatic pen in this key at the last bar of *Capriccio*, Strauss says: 'Is not this key of D♭ the best way of bringing to a close my life's work in the Theatre?'[1]

Capriccio was first performed in Munich during the Second World War, on October 28, 1942, with Viorica Ursuleac (Clemens Krauss's wife as well as Strauss's favourite soprano) in the character of the Countess. Krauss conducted and Rudolf Hartmann produced the opera.

Strauss was aware that *Capriccio* is a Festival opera 'an opera for special occasions . . . it will never be a general repertory work, although it does form a regular part of the annual Munich Festival' (*Observer*).

The Story of the Opera

At the close of the eighteenth century Paris was captured by the forceful personality of Gluck, whose fundamental reforms of operatic style were being propagated at that time and whose theories formed the subject of heated debates in all interested circles.

---

[1] *Richard Strauss*, by Ernst Krause, Leipzig, 1956, p. 393. (Author's translation.)

156

1775

At a party given by Countess Madeleine the much debated issue 'Poetry or Music?' becomes the subject of controversy. The brother of the Countess has planned to celebrate his sister's birthday by presenting several items of cultural interest, and the guests have been invited to pass an opinion on the several proposals for the envisaged birthday festivity. Two close friends—the musician Flamand and the poet Olivier—are expected to contribute to the day's controversy by presenting their own works.

An instrumental sextette composed by Flamand can be heard from the music-room. Both artists are now watching the Countess, who is strongly impressed by the lovely music, with intent interest. Flamand and Olivier both feel how much they have become rivals with regard to the eventual choice of the gifted and highly cultured woman, who is also very beautiful. Both are in love with her. The theatre director, La Roche, is having a nap during the sextette; when he awakens he talks to the two artists, and the fundamental differences of opinion are discussed. The Countess is rather emotional after having heard the music, and the Count teases her, advising her not to show too openly her liking for the handsome Flamand—in fact, he advises his sister in a friendly manner to 'detach the author from the work'. The gay answer of the Countess now discloses how little her brother favours music in general, that he has a strong prejudice in favour of the spoken word, and that he has a very distinct liking for the lovely actress Clairon. The Countess leaves the music room with her brother.

La Roche now leaves the room which is reserved for his company's theatrical performances. He discloses his plan to the Countess. It is his intention to present a grand *azione teatrale*, in which his entire company will take part. The arrival of the actress Clairon interrupts the growing controversy. Clairon asks Olivier, who has been one of her former admirers, about the end of one of his poems which had so far been unfinished. A new 'scene' is then presented by Clairon and the Count, who recite their parts in an improvised fashion. The words of a sonnet, written in honour of the Countess, are recited for the first time.

Olivier and Flamand remain together with the Countess. The poet once more recites his verses with much emotion, and does not fail to show his deep affection for the Countess. Flamand is greatly attracted by the beauty of the poem, and he feels inspired to compose something—he goes into the music room. Meanwhile the Countess is at pains to appease the extremely sentimental poet. Flamand re-enters with the music he has just written, which is intended to complement the sonnet.

The Countess is strongly impressed by the beauty of the words, which have been given much life by the music. Flamand now tells the Countess of his love for her and asks for an answer. She promises the musician that she will be in the library next morning at eleven, at which time she will announce her choice—the spoken word or the music; in other words, Olivier or Flamand.

Because of her natural inclination towards music the Countess unconsciously favours Flamand. His love for her is one which has a direct bearing on his work, but the relationship of Flamand to the object of his adoration is conditioned by his art; his love therefore is secondary.

Olivier's thoughts, on the other hand, centre around the Countess, and his masculinity confuses her. The poet's powerful and superior mind has another trend: to use these powers consciously in the quest of his love. It is obvious what this means. Before words have been formulated some thought must have preceded them. But in music it is different. Music is the most direct of all arts. The tune comes out of Space, the vastness of which no human mind can fathom. But the sound of this tune is—simultaneously—the very first thought *and* expression.

The Count returns in good humour talking enthusiastically about Clairon, who is said to have praised the Count's gifts as an actor. The Count's sister then teases him in a friendly manner about his affection for Clairon, but she also confesses that both Flamand and Olivier have succeeded in doing much to confuse her.

The company comes from the theatre. La Roche now surprises the company with a young dancer who delights the party.

Following the dance, Olivier and Flamond start a fresh argument about the spoken word and the tune, poetry and music. Olivier and the Count both agree in their refusal to admit that opera is an art.

La Roche for his part laments the 'terrific noise of the orchestras' in 'modern opera', as well as the disappearance of the 'art' song of the Italian school. Two Italian singers now sing a duet in the classical style, a style which La Roche believes to be most praiseworthy. . . . The discussion comes to a close.

The Count and Clairon plan a trip in the evening to Paris, and the Count is extremely happy at the prospects ahead of him.

The company in general now asks La Roche to disclose his plans for the envisaged birthday festivity. La Roche tells of his plan to present an allegory: 'The birth of Pallas Athene'. An outburst of laughter, especially from his rivals, Olivier and Flamand, at first appears to confuse and hurt La Roche. . . . The allegory was intended to be the first part of the theatrical performance, and now the Countess, trying to soothe his hurt feelings, asks La Roche what the second part of the performance is intended to present. To this question La Roche answers by explaining his second part, 'The birth of Pallas Athene'. He does this in a most bombastic way and his narrative is extremely theatrical and antiquated. The first reaction of the company is very antagonistic, but La Roche's enthusiasm for his own argument somehow overawes the company and by skilfully pointing out his own merits he manages to win over the party.

The Countess has a new idea. She proposes to the musician and to the poet that a new and mutual work should be written. Her brother is aghast at this proposal.

The Count has another idea. He maliciously proposes that the day's controversies ought to be made the subject of a new opera, he also states that all persons present should be impersonated in this opera. At first everybody is perplexed at the Count's idea, but soon the company gives him general support. The negative response of La Roche is overlooked. Olivier is willing to begin with his part of the work at once; he hopes to win the favour of the Countess, whose final decision for either Flamand or himself is to be expected at the close of the opera.

Clairon bids farewell to the company and leaves for Paris in company of the Count. The Countess retires. Flamand and Olivier glance at her as she leaves, both men are quite certain of their respective victory. La Roche prepares to leave, and while doing so, he gives some advice to Olivier about the proposed new poem.

The question as to whether the spoken word or the tune shall have priority is still an open matter. The Countess alone is entitled to pass judgment on this issue. Her decision will have a double meaning: to close the theoretical argument and to clarify her personal inclination.

The Countess's major-domo enters and tells his mistress that Olivier will be at the house next morning at eleven o'clock and that he will expect the final answer for the end of the opera.

The Countess is greatly astonished to realise that both rivals appear to her as an indivisible entity. She wishes to do all in her power to come to a decision. For that purpose she once more repeats the sonnet which was composed by Flamand. But she does not come to any decision. 'A vain attempt to detach one from the other. Both—the spoken word and the tune—are indivisible. Both have created something new. The great secret is the fact that one art has been redeemed by the other!'

> (*The German text of the above was written by Rudolf Hart-mann, and. the free translation of it is by William Mann.*)

Royal Opera House, Covent Garden
Visit of Bavarian State Opera
September 22 (British première) and 24, 1953, in German

Flamand	Holm
Olivier	Peter
La Roche	Kusche
Countess	Cunitz
Count	Schmitt-Walter
Clairon	Töpper
Major-Domo	Wieter
Conductor	Heger

Three performances of *Capriccio* were billed in London, but owing to the fact that the irreplaceable Benno Kusche contracted a throat infection shortly after his arrival, the first performance was postponed. It was not even known whether *Capriccio* could be given at all —it would depend on Mr. Kusche's recovery.

But fortunately he did recover sufficiently to allow two performances of the opera to take place, although he sung with some difficulty after his monologue. At the end of a dissertation on the opera itself in the *Sunday Times*, Ernest Newman declared that the production 'showed the style of the company at its finest. Robert Heger conducted, Rudolf Hartmann was the producer, and Benno Kusche and Maud Cunitz were most admirable as the Theatre Director and the Countess respectively.'

Since there is little action, in the dramatic sense during the course of the opera, the Royal Opera House provided the public with a written briefing on the complex story, so that they might be aware of what was taking place on the stage. As in *Ariadne* it was easy to follow the words since what seemed to be a chamber orchestra accompanied them 'until the end when the Countess yields to the claims of opera as a glorious art in its own right—then, but not before, the full orchestra soars, carrying the Countess's final monologue in its flight'.

Of the three available first line sopranos who included the Countess in their repertoires at the time, Maud Cunitz was considered by *The Times* to lack 'that last degree of sauvity and vocal enchantment that her sonnet demands, but she carried the part of the Countess with dignity and ease'. The same newspaper welcomed the reappearance of Robert Heger 'at the desk at which he last stood some twenty years ago'.[1]

The single set was charmingly designed and despite the requirements of the acting area, managed to look lived in. The lighting effect at the end of the opera is technically sure-fire: not difficult to achieve, but giving a stupendous effect.

The scene is never forgotten pictorially, and we can agree with Neville Cardus who said: 'Nobody has excelled him [Strauss] at the art of giving the finishing touch, the "once-upon-a-time" cadential flick that lends to comedy some gracious pathos of distance.' Here indeed, with his last operatic gesture, Strauss proved himself to be a great man of the theatre who, throughout his working life, had asked his librettists for nothing but the simplest works so that he might translate the story in terms of music and action for the spectators.

The Opera House, Glyndebourne

May 22, 24, 26, 30, June 1, 4, 9, 11, 13, 15, 1963, for ten performances in German

Flamand	Wilhelm
Olivier	Wolansky
La Roche	Kusche
Countess	Söderström
Count	Krause
Clairon	Cervena
Major-Domo	Shirley-Quirk
Conductor	Pritchard

Scenery: Dennis Lennon
Costumes: Anthony Powell

Producer: Günther Rennert

'Strauss Work finds an English home' was the heading of *The Times* music critic's notice for *Capriccio*, and he went on 'at Glyndebourne, whose festival theatre makes a perfect setting both within and without, for the civilized, gentle but never oppressively serious discussions that form the opera's substance'. (One might even contemplate their being held in the organ room there!)

[1] Robert Heger's last appearance had been on June 5, 1935, when he conducted Weinberger's *Schwanda the Bagpiper* at Covent Garden.

'*Capriccio* was intended to be played in one act; at Glyndebourne, thank heavens, they use the two-act version of the Bavarian State Opera' (*Observer*). 'John Pritchard's conducting is alert, expert in the main '(*Financial Times*), 'yet much of the playing and singing was far too loud. Of course the big . . . ensembles . . . need attack and gusto; and these Mr. Pritchard managed well enough. But had he read and taken to heart, we wondered, Strauss's preface to the score which is mainly concerned with verbal audibility . . .' (*Sunday Times*). 'But the big climax in the Countess's final monologue sounded superb, and by this time Mr. Pritchard (with Strauss's assistance) was avoiding the top-heavy orchestral balance which drowns words' (*The Times*).

'The great moments of the score . . . should ravish the listener's senses with a Silver Age distillation of beauty; and the rest is always interesting and ingenious enough to hold his attention, provided he has taken the wise precaution of familiarising himself with every twist and turn of the text' (*Sunday Times*) 'because in a conversation piece it is essential to know what the conversation is about. [Hence] verbal enunciation in this opera is of first importance' (*The Times*). 'I cannot think of an opera which more clearly needs to be performed in the language which the majority of the audience itself speaks' (*Guardian*).

'This Glyndebourne production, however, is too honest and too clear . . . [it] is anti-romantic. This showed itself in several ways—the smart "interior decoration" quality of Dennis Lennon's set; the slightly shabby appearance by the two young lovers; a Countess rather harder, less sentimental, than we are accustomed to—and generally in a lack of tenderness. It was a truthful presentation of the opera' (*Financial Times*).

'When the curtain rose and the sextet-overture continued from an inner room, the soft comments of Flamand (Horst Wilhelm) and Olivier (Raymond Wolansky) captured all the delicacy and clarity of this exquisite opening (*Sunday Times*), and when he awoke, they were joined by 'a genial Pickwickian La Roche (Mr. Benno Kusche, much mellowed since we last heard him in this role)' (*The Times*).[1] His 'impresario was much the most stylish performance' (*Observer*).

'The boyish character of the production is typified by Tom Krause's Count, admirably sung but portrayed as an infatuated teenager' (*The Times*). 'A fine baritone, [he] conveyed little impression of aristocratic style as he slouched around the stage with his cheerful modern grin' (*Sunday Times*). 'Tom Krause, the Count, has not yet mastered the conversational style, which the others managed well' (*Financial Times*).

As the actress Clairon (an historical character) 'Sona Cervena brought the right note of slight dramatic exaggeration to the part' (*Daily Telegraph*).

'The opera becomes progressively the leading soprano's evening' (*Guardian*). 'Miss Elisabeth Söderström started nervously, with an almost hysterical restraint that withheld the star quality which the Countess has to project' (*The Times*). She 'had great vocal charm but lacked the dignity and "distancing" needed for this reincarnation of the Marschallin' (*Daily Telegraph*). [She] 'seemed in the hurly-burly to miss much of the musical and dramatic distinction of the Countess's role until the final scene of all' (*Sunday Times*). 'Elisabeth

[1] Almost ten years before, in September 1953, at Covent Garden.

Söderström got the right note of tremulous rapture into her last scene' (*Observer*) 'where, left alone in the moonlight, she asks her heart to decide between the rivals. Here a certain hard archness which had marred the first half of Miss Söderström's performance fell away and she rose finely to the music's demands' (*Guardian*).

Summary of Performances

London .	.	.	2
Glyndebourne	.	.	10
			—
TOTAL	.	.	12

THE SILENT WOMAN

THE SILENT WOMAN

THROUGHOUT HIS PARTNERSHIP with von Hofmannsthal, Strauss's robust sense of humour had been kept in check by the poet, even in such a character as Baron Ochs. After the death of von Hofmannsthal, Strauss turned to his friend, Stefan Zweig, who submitted a very free version of Ben Jonson's *Epicoene* (with more than a little of *Don Pasquale* and an Italian opera troupe thrown in). This was put forward in period to 1780 and called—in English—*The Silent Woman*.

The collaboration was most successful and the opera was produced under enormous difficulties in Dresden in 1935. Politics obtruded since Zweig was a Jew, and his name was removed from the bills, just before the opening, by Hitler's own command. Strauss threatened to withdraw the opera unless Zweig was given his due credit, and so the name was re-instated.

But despite its artistic success *die Schweigsame Frau* was already doomed, and played for a mere four performances. It was withdrawn and did not appear again in Germany until 1947.

It is one of the least frequently staged of Strauss's operas, because of the extreme complexity of the score and the attendant difficulties in vocal casting.

The Story of the Opera

ACT I

In the London house of Sir John Morosus, a rich old retired admiral, his Housekeeper is busy dusting. There is a knock: it is Razorblade, the Barber, who had come to shave Sir John. The garrulous Housekeeper welcomes the chance of conversation, for in that house, Sir John insists on quiet everywhere and all the time. The Housekeeper resents it, but would not resent it at all if Sir John would marry her.

She hints as much to the Barber. If only he would suggest to Sir John. . . . But the Barber brushes the suggestion aside and gets more and more angry with her for detaining him. They quarrel violently and wake up Sir John who enters with a volley of nautical abuse for the Housekeeper—'You rotten, unseaworthy wreck!' She leaves.

As the Barber begins shaving him, Morosus complains of the noise that surrounds his house —shouting, street music, and, worst of all, 'the thousand bells of London'. Moreover, at home he must endure the babble of the Housekeeper. The Barber suggests that Sir John should get rid of her and marry a young, obedient, silent woman. Morosus is fiercely incredulous. Who ever heard of a silent woman?

But such a phenomenon does exist, the Barber assures him. And think of how comforting and cheering her company would be! The vision evidently appeals to Sir John, and the Barber sees possibilities for himself as a marriage-broker. But, Sir John objects, youth wants youth—'and quite right, too. No, no, I am too old'. Not at all, says the Barber. Maturity has its attractions.

> Gladly ev'ry wise man's daughter
> Weds a man whose ways are sure,
> For the poet well has taught her,
> 'Youth's a stuff will not endure.'

Suddenly, loud knocking interrupts them. Forcing his way past the Housekeeper, a young man appears. It is Henry, Sir John's long-lost nephew. The old man is overjoyed: here is an heir who can give him company. No bride will be needed. He will be delighted to welcome Henry's companions who wait below—until he finds out that they are not "troops" (as he first misheard) but a troupe of Italian opera singers led by Vanuzzi. Worse still, Henry discloses that he sings himself. His uncle is furious: 'A Morosus who sings is no Morosus!' And when Henry discloses that one of the singers, Aminta, is his wife, then Sir John curses the lot, disinherits Henry, and tells the Barber to bring his 'silent woman' with a parson and a lawyer next day. He storms out. The Barber explains that Sir John is a kind man really, though he was once blown up when a powder-magazine exploded (which accounts for his fanatical aversion to noise ever since). And (adds the Barber) what a huge fortune Henry is walking out of—fifty thousand pounds! The members of the troupe, in amazement, repeat the figure.

Aminta offers to leave Henry so as to enable him to stay. He refuses and proclaims his loyalty to the troupe. Well then, says the Barber, would one of the ladies of the troupe like to volunteer to be the silent young bride whom the Barber must fetch for Sir John tomorrow? Isotta and Carlotta show musically just why they could never bear such a fate.

Suddenly the Barber is seized, self-importantly, with an idea: a mock-marriage for Sir John, to a 'silent woman' who turns out to be a shrew, with the members of the troupe enacting the necessary roles! Then Sir John—when eventually he learns that the marriage was false—will be so relieved that he will welcome Henry back, 'entanglements' and all. The 'cast' for the impersonation is decided, and the Barber's inspiration is applauded by all, with many a bravo for Master Razorblade himself.

ACT II

The next afternoon Sir John is pulling on his best clothes for the wedding. The House-keeper, suspicious after having overheard something of the Barber's plot through the keyhole, attempts to warn Sir John, but he will have none of her.

The Barber enters with the announcement that he has three candidates for Sir John's hand. He asks Sir John not to intimidate the girls, each of them 'sweet and shy and new to passion'. The 'candidates' enter—Carlotta in disguise as a clumsy peasant, Isotta as a bluestocking,

Aminta as 'Timida', a demure, well-bred girl. Morosus rejects the first two, but 'Timida' captivates him: a sweet, unspoiled creature who likes to stay at home—

> Stitching the dreams that fill my head
> Into patterns of fine embroidery thread.

Old Sir John is genuinely touched—and so, despite herself, is Aminta (who becomes rather ashamed of duping such an evidently lovable old man). Then Vanuzzi, in disguise as a parson, and Morbio as a lawyer, enter. The 'marriage' is performed. A rapt moment that follows is shattered by the entry of Farfallo and others of the troupe, claiming to be old shipmates of Sir John's and insisting on celebrating his marriage. Sir John, angry, calls them a lying mob, but Farfallo opens a window and invites the neighbours to celebrate too. Sir John is reduced almost to apoplexy before they are induced to leave by the promise of free beer at a local inn.

But worse is to come when Sir John is left alone with his 'Timida'. Steeling herself to play the part, Aminta stamps, shouts and declares her intention to lead a life full of music and good cheer, and to have a parrot, too. Sir John, at first stupefied, eventually curses himself furiously for being such a fool. When Henry enters, Sir John begs him for protection against this 'devil'. Henry realistically forces Aminta into her chamber, tells his uncle to get some much needed sleep, and promises to arrange a legal annulment of the marriage next day. Meanwhile he promises to keep Aminta quiet. (And indeed, as loving husband to loving wife, he knows the way.)

ACT III

Next day the house has evidently been thrown into total disorder by 'Timida' (Aminta) who is now acting her part to the letter. She even has a parrot, as she threatened to have. She turns down Sir John's request, conveyed by the Housekeeper, for a little less noise, and proceeds to have a singing lesson with Henry as a disguised music-master and Farfallo as harpsichord accompanist. Morosus himself implores her mercy but she ignores him.

But all fall quiet when the Barber enters. He announces that the legal action to annul the marriage (a Consistory Court before a Chancellor and two assessors) will be held in a few minutes. But 'Timida' indignantly refuses the bribe that Sir John offers if she will voluntarily set him free. She claims that she still wants to be Lady Morosus and piles on the pretended pathos in a parody of folk-song style:

> Johnny is my love for ever
> I would die without his smile!
> Where he goeth I will follow
> Though it were ten thousand mile.

The legal gentlemen arrive (Vanuzzi as the judge, Farfallo and Morbio as assessors). With a mass of Latin mumbo-jumbo they try Sir John's petition, that he married under false pretences a woman who was not what she claimed to be. They produce witnesses (Carlotta, Isotta, and Henry, all in disguise) who allege that the bride has slept with another man

(Henry himself). It is the real Aminta, rather than the pretended Timida, who finds it difficult to deny that she loves this other man.

It appears that Sir John's case against the marriage is proved. But his rejoicing is premature. One of the assessors (Farfallo) dissents on the grounds that 'Timida's' virginity was not a condition of the marriage contract. The 'Court' agrees. The petition is refused.

Sir John Morosus—exhausted, ill, defeated—throws himself in despair on the bed. Then at a signal from the Barber the others reveal their deception. Aminta offers true, daughterly affection to Sir John. At first Sir John is furious. Then he starts to laugh. Why, if the troupe can act as well as this, he will even go to see them in opera!

Led by Vanuzzi, the troupe salute Sir John and sing the praise of music. Their play (and our opera) is near its end. One by one they depart, leaving Sir John at table with Henry and Aminta at his either side. He leans back at his ease and takes a long look at Aminta: 'A rare delight it is to find a silent, beautiful girl, but it is more delightful when she belongs to another man!'

ARTHUR JACOBS

Royal Opera House, Covent Garden
November 20, (British première), 22, 24, 28, 30, December 6, 1961, for six performances in English

Featherbed	Sinclair
Razorblade	J. Ward
Morosus	D. Ward
Henry	Macdonald
Vanuzzi	Kelly
Morbio	Ronald Lewis
Isotta	Vaughan
Carlotta	Berry
Farfallo	Langdon
Aminta	Holt
Conductor	Kempe

Designer: Martin Battersby   Producer: Franz Josef Wild

It may have been intentional or intuitive, or merely by personal inclination that von Hofmannsthal declined to provide Strauss with a truly comic libretto. The plot of *The Silent Woman* has more than a whiff of *Schadenfreude* and turns out to be very un-English in so far as the behaviour of the characters is concerned.

The first British performance (twenty-six years after the Dresden première) was received with mixed feelings. The musical difficulties communicated themselves through several of the singers who seemed to be insufficiently familiar with their parts. Andrew Porter in the *Financial Times* described the first night as 'a sketch for a very good performance'. This would seem a fair account since Desmond Shaw-Taylor in the *Sunday Times* went further by stating that 'There is more, far more, in *The Silent Woman* than this audience was allowed to suspect.'

A new soprano, Barbara Holt, was half-praised for what Philip Hope-Wallace in the *Guardian* described as 'a plucky shot at the demandingly elaborate and important part of the heroine . . .'. The production was severely criticised all round for its many dramatic weaknesses, and the set was considered to have an unlived-in and empty appearance. *The Times* found that 'two unrelated namesakes held the stage most forcibly, Mr. David Ward as the sensitive seadog, and Mr. Joseph Ward as the flouncing Figaro of London town . . .'.

The two heroes of the evening were undoubtedly Arthur Jacobs, with his witty and adroit translation (which seldom came across all the same) and Rudolf Kempe. Kempe handled the score and orchestra with his customary felicitious touch and 'realised the fine-fingered scoring with an exquisite delivery of tone and style'. The first performance was preceded by the huge number of twenty-four orchestral rehearsals, an event unprecedented at Covent Garden.

By the last three performances, the singers had gained considerably more confidence and Mr. Porter's 'very good performance' was realised.

A seventh performance, announced from the start for December 8, was cancelled because of David Ward's indisposition, and Cio-Cio San took the place of Aminta that night at Covent Garden.

Summary of Performances:

London . . . TOTAL 6

Appendices

APPENDIX A

Herein are records of three performances felt worthy of inclusion as they can all be described as 'live', in so far as they emanate from once-live occasions.

The 1926 *Rosenkavalier* film is a rarity, perhaps because the British National Film Archive holds only an incomplete file copy, which can never be publicly shown. The performance of Michael Bohnen and the atmosphere of a 1750 Vienna are carefully preserved and the film offers a most interesting complimentary piece to the opera.

The 1961 colour film of *Rosenkavalier* forms the second of these records.

And, lastly, the BBC's enterprising television production of *Salome* is described with quotations from contemporary press criticisms.

ROSENKAVALIER FILMED, 1926

Hofmannsthal and Strauss felt that a film of their most-performed work might help to stimulate further interest in it, and to provide them with extra royalties. In 1924 von Hofmannsthal wrote a script which treated the story 'in the manner of a novel: it introduces the characters, or for those who know them, tells something new of these old acquaintances. Nowhere (not even in the final scene) are the events of the opera exactly repeated—not in a single scene.' In early 1925 Strauss made a version of the opera score to be played as an accompaniment to the (silent) film, and after securing Robert Wiene as director, since, in von Hofmannsthal's opinion, he was '(next to Lubitsch) the only German film director who has acquired an international reputation and whose work is accepted in America'.[1]

The film went into production with Pan-Film AG of Vienna in the Spring of 1925 and it had its première, with Strauss conducting the orchestra, in the Opera House at Dresden on January 10, 1926.

The British première was on April 12, 1926, at the Tivoli Cinema, Strand, London. Strauss conducted the Tivoli Orchestra for the first showing only, but stayed in London to record the complete suite for H.M.V. at Queen's Hall. The cast was as follows, in order of appearance:

Baron Ochs von Lerchenau	Michael Bohnen
Octavian Rofrano	Jaque Catelain
The Marschallin	Huguette Duflos
The Field Marshall	Paul Hartmann

[1] Wiene was responsible for *The Cabinet of Dr. Caligari*, 1919.

Valzacchi	Frederich Feher
Annina	Carmen Cartellieri
Sophie	Elly Febie Berger
Faninal	Carl Forest

The film at the first performance was 9,000 ft. long. At subsequent showings it had been reduced to about 8,000 ft.

It was ably directed, and the close-ups which it allowed gave felicitous touches. Such a one as Octavian's look at the rose he held to Sophie, the symbolic rose which was at that moment very much between them, was most effective.

The film starts with a messenger riding the immense distance to Ochs's castle of 'four and twenty hours' by coach from Vienna, with the Marschallin's letter about Sophie. 'Baron Lerchenau of ancient lineage and almost indescribable poverty' is played by Michael Bohnen (who sang the part twice in 1914 at Drury Lane). The business with his legs, which he used to express delight, said more than words; and his foolish, yet not oafish face, gives a clue to the disputed question of how the part of Ochs should be characterised.

There is a flashback to the Marschallin's childhood in the Convent and her introduction to the Field Marshal, their marriage, and his leaving her on their wedding day to command the Emperor's Army. There follow many feet of battle scenes, since the Field Marshal figures largely in this version of the story.

The film ends with the unmasking of Ochs (as well as a duel between the Field Marshal and Octavian) in similar circumstances to those in the opera, but in Diana's Grotto at the country house of the Field Marshal, during a *fête masqué* given by the Marschallin. The Valzacchi and Annina characters in this version are considerably weakened because they undo their own mischief for reasons of conscience; and the Marschallin and her husband are reunited, how happily, von Hofmannsthal does not tell us.

There was a full attendance for the première of the film, and Strauss was accorded the honours 'more of a film-star than of a composer and conductor' (*The Times*). The 'solemn-looking elderly gentleman' (*The Times*) had composed one new number for the film, a march for the long sequence of the arrival of Octavian at the Faninal house for the presentation of the silver rose.

ROSENKAVALIER 1960 ENSHRINED

Dr. Paul Czinner's policy of preserving great dancers' and singers' interpretations for posterity was directed in 1960 towards that year's Salzburg Festival production of *Der Rosenkavalier*. The completed film was first shown at the Metropole Cinema, Bonn, on October 17, 1961, when the report stated that 'it assembles a fine cast (as good, one believes, as can be found in this imperfect world) in an uncut performance' (*The Times*).

The cast consists of:

Octavian	Jurinač
Marschallin	Schwarzkopf

Baron Ochs	Edelmann
Valzacchi	Ercolani
Annina	Rossel-Majdan
Tenor Singer	Zampieri
von Faninal	Kunz
Sophie	Rothenberger
Conductor	von Karajan

Scenery: Teo Otto   Producer: Rudolf Hartmann
Costumes: Erni Kniepert   Sound Recording: Edgar A. Vetter

The British première of the film took place on June 22, 1962, at the Odeon Cinema, Bath (during the Bath Festival) and it then moved to the Festival Hall, London, where it was shown on July 9 for one week, and then intermittently during 1962 and 1963.

The Times pointed out the felicities which the film has to offer: 'Miss Jurinač's Octavian. . . . Points of vocal characterization in Miss Schwarzkopf's handling of the Marschallin. . . . Miss Rothenberger's radiantly innocent Sophie. . . . Mr. Kunz [who] creates an archetypal social climber. . . . Mr. Edelmann's Ochs, a model of restraint.'

Indeed the whole production shows the greatest restraint and a feeling both for style and musical circumspection. No phrase is ever interrupted by a change of camera angle, nor do these angles, however limited, become dull or repetitive. It is only the occasional long-shot of an intimate scene which appears awkward.

There are some wonderful sets by Teo Otto which always manage to retain the feeling of opera rather than the studio, and the colour is very much better than one might expect from seeing the *Faninalische Programme* first.

One may question the need for accompanying the conductor to the rostrum before each act starts, and for brooding a little over the orchestra, rather like Disney did in the middle of *Fantasia*; but what did seem out of place was the description of Valzacchi and Annina as Spaniards. There is no precedent for this, and Strauss refers to them as 'the Italians',[1] in a letter to von Hofmannsthal.

But the film achieves its purpose most excellently, and at last there is a permanent record of a Strauss opera in sight and sound, a record, moreover, that is as authentic as one could hope for, within a dozen years of the composer's death.

SALOME TELEVISED 1957

BBC Television from Lime Grove
Performed and transmitted live on September 26, 1957

Narraboth	Nilsson
Jokanaan	Foster
Salome	Pilarczyk

[1] *Correspondence*, p. 46.

Herod	Eschert
Herodias	Sinclair
Conductor	Goehr

Designer: Norman James   Producer: Rudolf Cartier

Wardrobe Supervisor: Pamela Glanville

The BBC transmitted a live performance of the complete *Salome* in a newly supervised English translation, complete with sound—and visual—effects not possible in the opera house. The *Radio Times* gave its front cover to a picture of Salome (Helga Pilarczyk) and Herod (Jon Vickers), while the leading television article was specially commissioned from the musician and critic Arthur Jacobs. It was headed 'The Sensational *Salome*' and started: 'King Herod was wearing flannel trousers and a blue blazer; Salome was in a green woollen dress. . . .'

The producer was the successful Rudolph Cartier whose previous productions of opera on television had been praised; yet despite the use of 'the largest single stage set (69 ft. × 65 ft.) ever used in a television studio', and Cartier's inviting description of the culmination of the opera as 'the first strip-tease in history, the Dance of the Seven Veils', it cannot be considered an artistic success.

Cartier fell into many of the pitfalls which abound when a work designed for a large stage, and in this case without the merciful distance of the orchestra pit between audience and singers is transferred to the intimacy of the viewer's hearth. There were the needless vistas down singers' throats and unoperatically surprising scenes of the characters outside the conventional terrace. Cartier also made the cardinal error of having the head carried off *before* Herod ordered Salome's destruction.

But, on the credit side, Pilarczyk's performance was as effective as it had been at longer range in Edinburgh, and once one had become accustomed to the sound engineers constantly changing the levels of the voices, one realised that the use of an echo chamber behind Norman Foster's voice for the Prophet in the cistern was apt. Unfortunately Jon Vickers was unable to sing at the last moment, and Hasso Eschert was found in time to rehearse with the cameras and to learn a few vital phrases in English. The rest of the role he sung in his native German. This performance was tele-recorded for further use.

Whether the idea was worthwhile or not must depend upon who enjoyed watching at home on this and on the two further occasions when Tele-Salome has been transmitted. While the *Observer* felt that the opera was 'moderately well suited to the medium', this paper expressed some uneasiness at the thought of 'Salome lying on your own fireside, intoxicated with passion, staring into that gory face. . . .'

The Times summed up its appraisal coldly: 'the whole thing, enterprising as it was, seemed a mistake'.

APPENDIX B

BIBLIOGRAPHY

Beecham, Sir Thomas, Bart., *A Mingled Chime*. Hutchinson, 1944

Blom, Eric, *The Rose Cavalier*. Oxford, 1930

Cardus, Neville, *Sir Thomas Beecham*. Collins, 1961

Casti, Gianbattista, *Opere Varie Vol. V, Raccolta di Melodrammi giocosi*. Luigi Tenré, 1821

Del Mar, Norman, *Richard Strauss*. Volume I. Barrie and Rockliff, 1962

Dent, Edward J., *Opera*. Penguin Books, 1940

Geissmar, Berta, *The Baton and the Jackboot*. Hamish Hamilton, 1944

Grove's *Dictionary of Music and Musicians*. Macmillan, 1959

Kobbé's *Complete Opera Book*. Putnam, 1922

Krause, Ernst, *Richard Strauss*. Breitkopf und Härtel, 1956

Newman, Ernest, *Opera Nights*. Putnam, 1943

Reid, Charles, *Thomas Beecham*. Gollancz, 1961

Renner, Hans, *Die Wunderwelt der Oper*. Vier Falken Verlag, 1938

Rosenthal, Harold, *Two Centuries of Opera at Covent Garden*. Putnam, 1958

Roth, Ernst, *Richard Strauss: Stage Works*. Boosey and Hawkes, 1954

Scanzoni, Signe von, *Richard Strauss und seine Sänger*. Drucke zur Münchener Musikge-
schichte, 1961

Scholes, Percy, *Concise Oxford Dictionary of Music*. Oxford, 1952

Shaw, George Bernard, *How to become a Music Critic*. Rupert Hart-Davis, 1960

Strauss, Richard, *Recollections and Reflections*. Boosey and Hawkes, 1949

Strauss, Richard und Gregor, Joseph, *Briefwechsel 1934–49*. Otto Müller Verlag, 1955

Strauss, Richard and von Hofmannsthal, Hugo, *Correspondence*. Collins, 1961

Trenner, Franz, *Richard Strauss. Dokumente seines Lebens u. Schaffens*. Verlag CH Beck, 1954

The Theatre, Vol. VII, No. 73, March 1907

Ballet and Opera, Vols. VI–VIII; and *Opera*, Vols. I–XIII *passim*

Covent Garden Books No. 7

Glyndebourne Festival Programme Books, 1953-63

The Daily and Sunday Newspapers, the Weekly Magazines of the period, and the *Radio
Times*

INDEXES

INDEX OF SINGERS IN STRAUSS OPERAS